The Power of 24 Hours

Joe Remington

I0211713

The Power of 24 Hours

Copyright © 2024 by Joe Remington

Cover design by Joe Remington

PowerOf24Hours.com

Disclaimer: This book is a non-fiction work. The author has made every effort to ensure the accuracy of the information within, but the information is presented "as is" with no guarantee of completeness or accuracy. The author and publisher shall have neither liability nor responsibility to any person or entity with respect to any loss or damage caused, or alleged to have been caused, directly or indirectly, by the information contained in this book.

Table of Contents

INTRODUCTION 1

The Library of Lost Hours 6

RITUALS OF THE RISING SUN 13

The Maze of Morning Miracles....................................28

THE FOCUS FRONTIER 33

The Forest of Focused Fortitude...................................46

MOTIVATE YOUR MINDSET 61

The Peaks of Purposeful Progress 84

YOUR MIDDAY MOMENTUM 95

Summit of Sustained Success................................. 109

THE ART OF TIME MASTERY 116

The Maze of Quick Conquests 129

THE POWER OF SAYING NO 137

The Desert of Decisive Denial 143

CONNECT & UNWIND.. 152

The Twilight of Connection.................................... 162

YOUR 24-HOUR BLUEPRINT............................... 169

Beyond the 24th Hour 175

FOREWORD

———

H ave you ever reached the end of a day wondering where all your time went? Time often slips away, leaving us scrambling to catch up. Yet, each day offers a powerful gift: 24 hours to shape our lives.

The Power of 24 Hours transcends typical time management. It's a guide to enriching your life with purpose, passion, and peace. Within these pages, you will discover how to transform each moment into a steppingstone toward your greatest goals.

Shattering Limiting Beliefs

Many of us believe we need more time for our goals, that our days are too short, or that time management means sacrificing joy. These beliefs paralyze us and leave us feeling helpless. The key isn't chasing more time but mastering the time we have. This book will help you break these mental barriers and embrace a new perspective on time.

The Gift of 24 Hours

We all have 24 hours each day. The secret to a fulfilling life is aligning these hours with our values and dreams. Imagine discovering that one belief or "Big Domino" that, once tipped, brings everything else into alignment. Here, that idea is mastering our use of time. This shift in perspective helps us fill our lives with what truly matters.

Realizing the True Worth of Time

Hindsight often reveals missed opportunities. We typically grasp time's value only after it's gone. This book guides you from regret to proactive engagement, transforming each moment into an opportunity for meaning and fulfillment.

From Realization to Action

Within the pages of The Power of 24 Hours, you're invited on a profound journey that will reshape your relationship with time. This isn't just another self-help book; it's a transformative experience that goes beyond theory to create lasting change in your life.

Imagine standing at the crossroads of your life, where each path represents a different way of using your precious 24 hours. As you progress through this book, you'll gain insights that illuminate these paths, revealing possibilities you may have never considered. But we won't stop at knowledge alone.

What sets this book apart is its commitment to turning realization into action. Through a unique combination of in-depth chapters and immersive adventures, you'll not only learn about time mastery but experience it firsthand. This dual approach ensures that the principles you learn don't just stay on the page but become an integral part of how you navigate your days.

Chapters and Adventures:

This book's unique structure combines two powerful elements to guide your transformation:

The Chapters: Will dive deep into your mind, unlocking time management secrets and shattering limiting beliefs. You'll confront common myths about time scarcity, busyness, and work-life balance, replacing them with empowering truths.

You'll discover transformative strategies that will revolutionize your relationship with time:

- As the sun rises, the RISE Framework energizes your mornings, setting a powerful tone for the day ahead.
- Fueled by this strong start, the FOCUS Framework sharpens your mind, helping you achieve peak productivity when it matters most.
- The MOTIVATE Framework keeps you driven and aligned with your goals throughout the day.
- The TIME Mastery Framework optimizes your routine for maximum efficiency and effectiveness.
- The THRIVE Framework ensures sustained performance and well-being, even during challenging times.
- As evening approaches, the CONNECT Framework helps you wind down, rejuvenating your spirit and strengthening your relationships.

These frameworks aren't isolated tools, but a symphony of strategies working in harmony. Together, they create a comprehensive system for time mastery, empowering you to make the most of every moment, from sunrise to sunset and beyond.

The Adventures: Will serve as your personal proving ground. These aren't mere thought experiments; they're vivid, engaging experiences that challenge you to apply the principles you've just learned in simulated real-life scenarios.

Your journey will take you through a series of transformative experiences, each designed to challenge and inspire you:

- You will wander through the dusty shelves of the Library of Lost Hours, where you'll confront the true value of time.
- Explore the vast Field of Insights into Time, unlocking profound revelations about your relationship with the clock.
- Navigate the twisting paths of the Maze of Morning Miracles, discovering the power of purposeful beginnings.
- You will brave the dense Forest of Focused Fortitude, honing your concentration amidst a world of distractions.
- Traverse the Maze of Quick Conquests, learning to seize opportunities and make every moment count.
- Cross the barren Desert of Decisive Denial, mastering the art of saying 'no' to protect your priorities.
- You will experience the Twilight of Connection, finding renewal in meaningful relationships and restful evenings.
- And finally, you will go Beyond the 24th Hour, putting all that you've learned to the test as your journey continues.

Each adventure builds upon the last, weaving together to create a rich tapestry of experiences that will fundamentally reshape your perception and use of time.

Redefining Success

Changing how you see time isn't always easy. We often carry misconceptions that hold us back, creating a cycle of stress and dissatisfaction. This book challenges these old ideas, helping you see time in a new way, focusing on what's important and making the most of every moment.

Throughout your journey, you'll confront and dismantle common limiting beliefs:

Myth 1: "I don't have enough time." As you progress through the chapters and adventures, you'll discover that time isn't as scarce as you think. The RISE and FOCUS Frameworks will shift your mindset from scarcity to abundance, teaching you to identify time-wasters and prioritize tasks that truly matter. Say goodbye to constant urgency and anxiety, and hello to a more purposeful use of your hours.

Myth 2: "Being busy means I'm doing well." The MOTIVATE and TIME Mastery Frameworks will help you debunk the busy equals productive equation. You will learn to distinguish between mere activity and true effectiveness. No more simply reacting to demands; instead, you'll proactively shape your life for meaningful progress.

Myth 3: "Work-life balance is impossible." The THRIVE and CONNECT Frameworks will help you redefine balance altogether. You'll learn it's not about equal time distribution, but about aligning actions with values. You'll discover how to seamlessly integrate your professional and personal goals, creating a harmonious and fulfilling life that works for you.

As you progress through the chapters and embark on the adventures, you'll uncover powerful truths and gain tools to overcome these limiting beliefs. But that's just the start. The insights and strategies you'll discover will transform how you perceive and use time, making every moment count in ways you never imagined possible.

By the time you reach "Beyond the 24th Hour," you'll have not only dismantled these myths but built a new, empowering relationship with time. You'll be equipped to redefine success on your own terms, creating a life of purpose, balance, and fulfillment.

Who Is This Book For?

This book is for anyone who feels like there's never enough time in the day. It's for those who want more than just to survive from one day to the next. If you've ever dreamed of a life where time works for you instead of against you, this book is for you.

Maybe you're trying to juggle work and family life. Perhaps you have big dreams you're working towards. Or maybe you just want your days to feel more meaningful. Whatever your situation, "The Power of 24 Hours" offers a new way to look at and use your time.

This book is especially helpful for three types of people who are ready to change how they think about and use their time:

Action-Oriented Dreamers: If you have big dreams and the drive to make them a reality, then this book is your catalyst for transformation. You'll find practical tools to seamlessly integrate your dreams into your daily routine, turning lofty goals into concrete achievements. Here, you'll learn how to bridge the gap between vision and action, ensuring your dreams don't remain mere wishful thinking.

Pragmatic Visionaries: Because, while many can dream, it takes true courage to believe in and pursue those dreams. If you're ready to turn your dreams into reality, then you've come to the right place. "The Power of 24 Hours" is your roadmap to turning imagination into achievement, guiding you with purpose and consistency toward the future you envision.

Balance Seekers: If you believe that real success means doing well at work and being happy in your personal life, then this book is for you. You'll learn how to build a life where your job and personal happiness work together, not against each other. The ideas in this book will help you succeed without giving up the things that make you happy. You'll find ways to do well at work while also enjoying your life outside of it.

In essence, "The Power of 24 Hours" is for anyone ready to take control of their time, align their actions with their goals, and create a life of purpose, balance, and fulfillment. Whether you're looking to supercharge your productivity, find harmony between work and life, or simply make the most of every day, this book provides the tools and insights you need to succeed.

Your Journey Begins Now

As you stand on the threshold of transformation, recognize that every page you turn is a step towards reclaiming your time and reshaping your destiny. "The Power of 24 Hours" isn't just a guide—it's a catalyst for profound change, empowering you to transform mere minutes into moments of significance.

Picture a life where each hour propels you towards your dreams, where your schedule aligns with your deepest values, and where time becomes your most powerful ally. This isn't a distant possibility—it's the reality awaiting you on the other side of these pages. The journey to a life brimming with purpose, achievement, and joy doesn't begin in some vague future.

It starts now, with the turn of this page. This moment marks the beginning of your transformation. Are you ready to unlock the full potential of your 24 hours? Can you envision a version of yourself that's more focused, fulfilled, and free? That person is within your reach, waiting to emerge through the practices and principles you'll discover in this book.

Take a deep breath. Center yourself.

As you turn the page, you step into a new reality—one where you command your time, rather than being ruled by it. Your 24-hour adventure to a brand new you begins right now. Remember, the clock is ticking, but now each second is an opportunity. Let's make every moment count. Your journey to mastering the power of 24 hours starts here.

INTRODUCTION

———

Welcome to "The Power of 24 Hours." I'm Joe Remington, and I'm honored you've chosen to join me on this transformative journey.

You've already glimpsed the exciting adventure ahead – the frameworks, challenges, and potential for profound change. But before we dive in, I want to share why this journey is deeply personal to me, and why I believe it has the power to revolutionize your life.

A Moment of Awakening

The evening started like any other. I stepped through the door, greeted by the warmth of a home-cooked meal and the familiar chatter of my then four-year-old daughter, Abby. Her eyes sparkled with the excitement of her day.

Suddenly, the piercing squeal of the weather radio cut off Abby's joyful chatter mid-sentence. Her eyes widened with concern. "Oh no! It's not another tornado, is it Daddy?" she asked, her voice concerned, with the memory of a recent storm still fresh in her mind.

I reached for her hand, about to reassure her, when I realized this wasn't a weather alert. As the message came across, a chill ran down my spine. A child, not much older than our Abby, had been abducted not far from us.

The police were seeking help, and time was of the essence. My wife, wooden spoon still in hand, turned from the stove with an expression mirroring my own concern.

We've always made it a point to be honest with Abby, breaking down the world's complexities in ways she can understand. This approach has nurtured a deep awareness and empathy in her, well beyond her years. As we carefully explained the situation, I saw Abby's expression change before my eyes. Her brow furrowed *(she gets that from her Mom)*, her lips pressed together in concentration.

Then, without hesitation, she looked up at us with eyes full of determination and said, "Let's pray right now Mommy and Daddy. "For the next ten minutes, this little girl prayed with a fervor and compassion that left us in awe. Tears streamed down our faces as we listened to her earnest pleas for the safety of a child she'd never met.

Dinner cooled on the stove, forgotten in the face of this moment of pure innocence, colliding with the harsh realities of the world. Two days later, as we were visiting my Mom after church, we heard that the missing child had been found safe. Relief washed over us.

Then, Abby looked up at us and asked a question that would change everything: "Daddy, what can we do to help the children that don't get found?" In that instant, time seemed to stand still. The true value of time hit me hard. I realized how important it is to use every second wisely, with purpose and compassion.

This book, in part was born from that realization – a tool not just for managing time, but for infusing each moment with meaning and purpose. It's a guide to help us all make the most of the precious time we have, inspired by a child's innocent wisdom and a father's awakening to the power of presence.

As you read these pages, I invite you to remember Abby's question. Let it be a catalyst for your own journey towards mastering your time, not just to do more, but to be more – more present, more purposeful, and more aligned with what truly matters in your life.

The Daily Quest of a Rock Alchemist

My awakening to the true value of time didn't end with Abby's profound question. It was just the beginning of my own hero's journey - one that I believe many of you will recognize in your own lives.

Like so many others, I'm caught in the timeless struggle between career and family. I'm in the specialty field of Quality Control, or what I like to call Rock Alchemy for an Aggregate and Paving Company. *My job quite literally rocks!*

It's a blend of fun and fulfillment, but the reality is that this crucial work keeps me away from home for long, demanding hours. It's a challenge many of us face — providing for our families often means sacrificing precious moments with them.

Imagine this: It's 4:30 in the morning, and while the world sleeps, I'm gearing up for an hour-long drive, ready to "rock and roll" out on my daily quest. Day after day, this journey sparked a transformation within me. My drive to work became my university on the go, where I listened to productivity, time management, and high-performance audiobooks, changing my mindset, skill set, and perspective.

I realized that to be the father and husband I aspire to be, I had to master not just the science of asphalt but the art of time itself.

This quest for time mastery isn't unique to me. Whether you're commuting to an office, traveling for work, or burning the midnight oil to build your dream, you likely know the ache of missing bedtime stories, family dinners, or simple moments of connection. But what if I told you that even with the demands of a career that keeps you away, you can still create a life rich in presence and purpose?

You see, like many of you, I wear multiple hats. I'm not just pursuing a career but building a legacy. I'm a husband nurturing a partnership, a father shaping the future, an aspiring author with stories to tell, and an individual with dreams that refuse to be silenced. In the precious few hours between coming home and going to bed late, I'm determined to honor each of these roles.

So, for me, and perhaps for you too, time management isn't just about productivity - it's about presence. It's about being fully there for my daughter Abby when we read together before bed, regardless of the day's challenges. It's about creating space for meaningful conversations with my wife, who dedicates her days to homeschooling our daughter. It's about carving out moments to pursue my passion for writing, like the book you're reading right now.

This juggling act might sound familiar to you. Maybe you're a parent trying to balance a career with family life. Perhaps you're a student working full-time while pursuing your degree. Or you could be an entrepreneur working too hard to bring your vision to life. Whatever your story, I bet you've felt the pressure of time weighing on your shoulders.

But here's what I've learned, and what I hope to share with you through this book: We are all heroes in our own stories, facing the dragon of time each day. And like any hero, we have the power to rise to the challenge.

My wife and I made a commitment to give Abby opportunities we never had, to prepare her for a world that's changing faster than we can imagine. This commitment forced me to reevaluate how I use every minute of my day. It pushed me to find ways to be more efficient at work, more present at home, and more intentional in my personal growth.

Through trial and error, successes and failures, I've discovered strategies and mindsets that have transformed my relationship with time. These discoveries form the core of "The Power of 24 Hours."

Beyond Time Management

The Power of 24 Hours isn't about cramming more into your day or optimizing every second. It's about something far more profound – it's about aligning your time with your deepest values and most cherished goals.

If you're feeling overwhelmed, it's easy to think you are just not cut out for effective time management. But here's the truth: the issue isn't time itself. It's about making conscious choices about what deserves your attention and energy.

This book is your invitation to fundamentally shift how you perceive and use time in every aspect of your life. It's about transforming time from a relentless taskmaster into a canvas for your personal and professional growth, a tool for crafting a life full of purpose and success.

As we embark on this journey together, remember; this isn't just about managing your schedule. It's about reshaping your relationship with time itself, unlocking new opportunities for growth, success, and personal fulfillment.

Are you ready to join me on this quest? Let's embark on this journey together and discover the power that lies within your 24 hours.

The Library of Lost Hours

———

The morning sun peeks through your blinds, painting your room in a soft, golden light. It seems like the start of just another day—until your phone's alarm shatters the peaceful silence.

The day begins, but something feels different.

Your hand moves automatically to silence it, fingers hovering over the snooze button on the screen. But you pause. Something feels different. There's a subtle shift in the air, a tingling sensation that makes you hesitate.

As you lie there, contemplating whether to get up, a deep rumble, like distant thunder, fully rouses you. Didn't you promise yourself you would get up early today? With a mix of determination and reluctance, you pry your eyes open, expecting to see your familiar, slightly messy bedroom.

Instead, you blink in disbelief.

Reality shifts, and you find yourself in a room of endless knowledge.

You're sitting in the middle of what looks like the biggest library you have ever seen. Bookshelves tower above you, stretching so high you can't see where they end. Books of every shape and color fill these shelves, some looking ancient, others brand new.

"Okay, I must still be dreaming," you mutter, but the pinch you give yourself feels all too real. The air smells like old books and leather, reminding you of a cozy antique shop, blended with the comforting aroma of your favorite library. And there is a sound, a constant ticking that seems to come from everywhere at once, as if you're inside a giant clock.

Each book holds a story - perhaps your story.

Curious despite your confusion, you stand up and start walking. Your hand trails along the book spines as you pass. Each one feels important somehow, like it's waiting for you to pick it up. You pull out a random book, its cover a deep blue. Opening it, you gasp. It's about you—but not quite. It's a story of what your life could have been if you'd made different choices.

A chill runs down your spine as questions flood your mind. What is this place? Why are you here? And what do all these books mean?

The whispers of doubt begin their assault.

As you explore, the temperature drops suddenly, sending a shiver down your spine. A voice, smooth and enticing, whispers from the shadows: "Why rush? Isn't your comfort more important than your dreams? Why sacrifice today's ease for tomorrow's uncertain rewards?" It's Procrastination, preying on your deepest fears.

The battle against your inner thoughts begins.

Surrounded by the lingering echoes of missed opportunities, Procrastination's voice grows louder: "How many times have you started, only to fail? Why do you want to risk another disappointment? Isn't it safer to dream rather than to do?" Its words cut deep, echoing the fears you've wrestled with countless times before.

Then, Self-Doubt slithers in, its voice sharp and undermining: "Who are you to think you can change? Remember all the times you've tried and given up? What makes this time any different?" It chips away at your resolve, making you question every ambition you've ever held.

The temptation of inaction looms large.

Laziness follows, its touch deceptively comforting: "Haven't you earned a rest? Why push yourself when you can just be content? Is the struggle worth it?" It paints a seductive picture of effortless contentment, hiding the true cost of inaction.

These voices weave a suffocating web of discouragement. They press in, a suffocating weight that makes it hard to breathe, to think, to hope. Your dreams and ambitions feel like they're slipping through your fingers, shrinking in the face of these doubts. Each passing second feels like another chance lost, another "what if" added to the pile of regrets.

A spark of defiance ignites within you.

But then, just as despair threatens to overwhelm you, a spark ignites within. A clear, defiant thought cuts through the chaos:

"What if today is the day everything changes? What if the person you are meant to become is waiting on the other side of this challenge? What will you regret more: the discomfort of trying, or the ache of never knowing what could have been?"

The power to choose your path reveals itself.

You've come to the realization that Procrastination, Self-Doubt, and Laziness aren't external enemies; they are internal voices that have become too dominant. They function like a broken compass, slowly guiding you off your true path through a series of small, insignificant choices. These mental habits thrive on your moments of hesitation, gaining strength each time you allow them to lead.

The real issue isn't whether you can silence these voices—you've always had that power. The true challenge lies in your readiness to take back control, to override this broken compass, and chart a course toward realizing your full potential.

The moment of truth arrives.

In this moment of clarity, you face the ultimate question: "Who do you want to be: the person who succumbs to fear and comfort, or the one who rises to meet their destiny?"

The choice, as it has always been, is yours.

Empowerment surges through you as clarity dawns.

Your mind clears as the fog of doubt lifts. You understand that the library, with its towering shelves and ticking clocks, reflects your inner world—a place where time can be lost or reclaimed. You feel a surge of determination, a resolve to not let another hour slip away. The control is yours, and with it, the power to shape your destiny.

This realization invigorates you. Each deep breath fills you with strength and pushes out fear. The doubts begin to fade, and your vision clears. Your heart steadies, fueled by a new, strong resolve. The once overpowering voices now seem distant and weak, their hold on you loosening.

A new chapter of your life begins to unfold.

With every breath, you feel more in control. The library, once a maze of confusion, now feels like a place of endless possibilities. The clock's ticking, once a reminder of lost time, now marks the rhythm of a new beginning. You see your goals clearly, and the path to achieving them is no longer obscured by doubt and fear.

Each step you take is firm and confident. The weight of procrastination, self-doubt, and laziness lifts off your shoulders. You feel lighter, freer. The library transforms from a prison of lost hours to a sanctuary of potential and opportunity.

With a renewed sense of purpose, you stand taller. The air crackles with the energy of impending change. The once oppressive atmosphere now feels charged with possibility, as if the very air around you is vibrating in anticipation of the steps you will take. You breathe in deeply, feeling the weight of past doubts lift, replaced by an electric sense of empowerment. Your eyes scan the shelves, not with a sense of being overwhelmed, but with the excitement of endless opportunities waiting to be explored.

You become the author of your own story.

In the Library of Lost Hours, you start writing your story. Each hour becomes a step toward the life you've always dreamed of. You pull a blank book from the shelf, its pages inviting you to fill them with your aspirations and plans. As you begin to write, the clock's ticking syncs with your heartbeat, each moment a testament to your commitment to change.

Transformation complete, you step into a new reality.

This journey of self-discovery transforms you into a master of your time, ready to make every second count. You leave the library changed, confident in your ability to create a life full of meaning and achieve the greatness you've always felt within you. The library door closes behind you, but the lessons learned, and the strength gained remain with you. Every tick of the clock now propels you forward, each second a chance to build the future you envision.

The next chapter of your journey beckons.

With this newfound clarity and resolve, you step into your day, knowing that you have the power to shape your destiny. Every hour is an opportunity, and you are ready to seize it, turning the once daunting prospect of time into a canvas for your life's masterpiece.

As you return to your familiar surroundings, a question lingers in your mind: How can you harness this newfound energy and purpose to transform the very start of your day? You realize that your mornings hold untapped potential—a chance to set the tone for the hours that follow.

A new dawn of possibility awaits.

The first rays of sunlight peek through your window, and with them comes an epiphany. Your journey towards mastering time doesn't begin when you step out the door or sit down at your desk. It starts the moment you open your eyes.

You feel a surge of anticipation. What if you could create a morning routine that not only prepares you for the day ahead but also aligns with your deepest values and goals? The prospect is both exciting and a little daunting.

As you ponder this, you sense that the next chapter of your journey is about to unfold. It promises to reveal the secrets of those who have mastered their mornings, turning the break of dawn into a powerful catalyst for success and fulfillment.

The adventure continues, and you're ready to rise.

With a mixture of curiosity and determination, you prepare to dive into the "RITUALS OF THE RISING SUN." You know that within its pages lie the keys to unlocking the full potential of your day's first hours—and by extension, the rest of your waking moments.

The clock ticks steadily, marking the passage of time. But now, instead of feeling pressured by its rhythm, you feel invigorated. You're ready to greet each new day not with dread or indifference, but with purpose and enthusiasm.

Your adventure in the Library of Lost Hours has shown you the value of time. Now, you're about to discover how to make the most of every moment, starting with the very first one. A new chapter is dawning with the rising sun—are you ready to embrace it?

RITUALS OF THE RISING SUN

"With every sunrise, a blank canvas is presented; let your rituals sketch a day filled with achievements and peace."

I magine waking up each day with a sense of excitement and purpose. Instead of rushing through your mornings, you have a structured approach that not only energizes you but also aligns your daily actions with your long-term goals. For me, rising before dawn each day, I've learned firsthand the power of a purposeful morning routine.

The RISE Framework, which is (REVITALIZE, INFUSE, STRATEGIZE, and EXECUTE), is designed to help you harness the potential of each new day, turning routine into ritual, and mundane mornings into moments of joy and productivity.

In my journey from chaos to clarity, I've discovered that the way we start our day sets the tone for everything that follows. Whether you're preparing for a day at the quarry like me, heading to an office, or working from home, a powerful morning routine can be your secret weapon for success.

Today is different because you're about to discover the transformative power of a purposeful morning routine. The RISE Framework will revolutionize how you start each day, setting you up for unprecedented success and fulfillment.

In this chapter, we'll delve into the building blocks of a truly productive day. We'll explore the tangible elements that can transform your mornings from something you endure to something you genuinely benefit from and enjoy. It's about crafting a day that not only moves you forward in your career but also leaves you feeling good about how you've spent your time - allowing you to be fully present for those bedtime stories and family moments we cherish so much.

So, let's explore these foundational elements together and start building days that are as productive as they are meaningful. Are you ready to wake up like never before?

The Power of a New Beginning

Each sunrise brings a unique opportunity to reset and renew. This daily renewal is a powerful concept: no matter what happened yesterday, today is a new chance to make progress, to grow, and to live intentionally. The beauty of mornings lies in their potential to set the tone for the entire day. By crafting a morning routine that aligns with your personal values and goals, you can create a foundation of positivity and purpose that influences everything you do.

Think about it: How often have you found that a good morning leads to a good day? It's not just anecdotal. Studies have shown that our morning mood and activities can have a significant impact on our productivity, creativity, and overall well-being throughout the day.

For instance, a study published in the Academy of Management Journal found that starting the day with a positive mindset leads to better engagement at work and higher job satisfaction. Another study from the Journal of Applied Psychology discovered that employees who experienced positive emotions in the morning were more likely to still be in a good mood throughout the day and provide better customer service.

But the power of mornings isn't just about mood, it's about setting intentions and taking control of your day before the world starts making demands on your time and energy. By setting up a morning routine, you're essentially creating a buffer between sleep and the chaos of daily life, giving yourself time to center your thoughts, energize your body, and prepare your mind for the challenges ahead.

Moreover, consistent morning rituals can help regulate your body's natural circadian rhythms, leading to better sleep patterns and improved overall health. The regularity of a morning routine can provide a sense of stability and control, which is especially valuable in our often unpredictable and stressful world.

As we explore the RISE Framework, keep in mind that the goal isn't to create a rigid, one-size-fits-all routine. Instead, it's about discovering what works best for you—what energizes you, what inspires you, and what helps you feel prepared and excited for the day ahead.

Your morning routine should be as unique as you are, tailored to your personal goals, lifestyle, and preferences. Remember that the path isn't always straight. You may encounter doubts, setbacks, and unexpected challenges. Embrace these as opportunities for growth and self-discovery.

With the potential of mornings clear, let's explore a structured approach to harness this power.

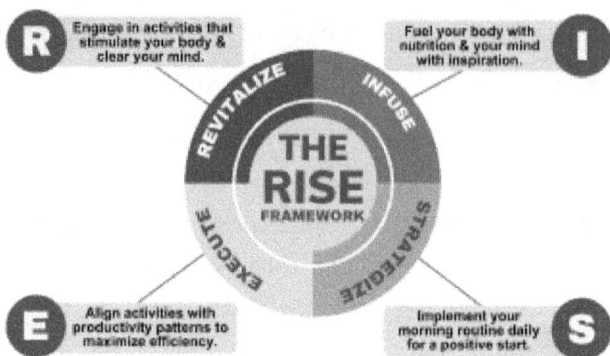

The RISE Framework:

To help you rise every morning and conquer your day, let's introduce each part of the RISE Framework:

1. Revitalize: Energize your mind, body, and spirit
2. Infuse: Add purpose and meaning to your mornings
3. Strategize: Plan your day for maximum effectiveness
4. Execute: Put your morning plan into action

By applying the RISE Framework—Revitalize, Infuse, Strategize, and Execute—you'll transform your mornings from a rushed blur into a powerful launchpad for your day. Each component builds upon the last, creating a comprehensive approach to morning mastery.

Now let's break down each part of the RISE Framework:

R – Revitalize - Mind, Body, & Spirit

Waking up is more than just ending sleep; it's about igniting your entire being—body, mind, and spirit. Revitalizing is a holistic awakening, a comprehensive activation that goes far beyond a mere physical warm-up.

Imagine beginning your day not just awake but truly alive, with every part of you energized and aligned for the day ahead. Whether it's through stretching, prayer and meditation, or a gratitude practice, revitalizing your morning sets the tone for a day lived with intention and vibrancy.

Think of waking up as a transition from rest to readiness, where every element of your being is prepared to engage with the world. This is the moment where you lay the foundation for everything that follows. It's about creating a state of alertness and positivity that fuels your entire day.

Here's How to Start Strong:

1. **Physical Activity:** Begin by getting your body moving. Physical activity can be as simple as stretching, a short walk, or a quick workout. This movement wakes up your muscles and boosts your circulation, helping to shake off sleepiness and prepare your body for the day's demands.

2. **Mindfulness and Focus:** After invigorating your body, center your mind. Calm your thoughts through mindfulness practices. This could be a deep breathing exercise, focusing on the rhythm of your breath, or reflecting on what you're grateful for.

3. **Spiritual Connection:** Nourish your spirit by connecting with God through prayer and reading Scripture first thing in

the morning. This allows you to align your heart and mind with eternal truths, setting a firm foundation for your day.

Each of these elements, physical activity, mindfulness, and spiritual connection, work together to create a powerful morning routine. They ensure you wake up fully, not just physically but mentally and spiritually as well. By the time you've completed these steps, you're not just awake; you're alive, vibrant, and ready to face the day with energy, intention, and a deep sense of purpose rooted in your faith.

Exercise: For the next week, commit to a 15-minute morning revitalization routine. Choose one activity for your body (like stretching), one for your mind (like deep breathing), and one for your spirit (like gratitude journaling).

Remember, the goal of revitalization is not perfection but progress. Even small steps towards a more intentional morning can lead to significant improvements in your daily life. As you continue to refine your revitalization routine, you'll discover what works best for you, creating a personalized approach to starting each day with vitality and purpose.

After fully waking up, it's time to make your morning even better by adding things that really matter to you.

I – INFUSE Your Mornings

This INFUSE phase is about enriching your morning with personal and meaningful elements. Whether it's savoring a cup of coffee in silence, journaling, or listening to a podcast, infusing your morning with these elements transforms it from routine to ritual, making each start something to cherish.

This is where you move from merely waking up to truly living in the moment. Infusing your morning turns it into a time of enjoyment and personal growth, dedicated to activities that resonate with your soul and set a positive tone for the entire day. It's about creating an environment and routine that feels like a gift to yourself, a daily celebration of your life and aspirations.

Here's How to Create a Morning That You Love:

1. **Focus Zone:** Establish a special place dedicated to your morning rituals. Whether it's a quiet corner of your room, a cozy chair by the window, or a specific spot at your table, create a space where you can concentrate and feel good.

2. **Light and Layout:** The way you arrange your space can significantly affect your mood and productivity. Good lighting, both natural and artificial, makes a big difference in how you feel.

3. **Sensory Boosts:** Engage your senses to enhance your morning experience. Incorporate elements like your favorite scent, such as calming lavender or invigorating citrus, through candles, or some essential oils. Play background music that uplifts you or sets a peaceful tone, whether it's classical, jazz, or nature sounds.

Imagine your morning beginning with fresh coffee aroma, soft music, and warm sunlight. You settle into your focus spot, feeling calm and comfortable. This is your special start, and it's filled with things that inspire and delight you.

Exercise: Create a morning playlist of songs or podcasts that inspire and motivate you. Listen to it for a week during your morning routine and note how it affects your mood and productivity.

Reflection: What activities or elements could you add to your morning that would make you look forward to waking up? How can you make your mornings feel less like a chore and more like a gift to yourself?

Remember, infusing your mornings with purpose is about more than just adding pleasant activities to your routine. It's about creating a mindset of intentionality and appreciation that carries through your entire day. By taking the time to make your mornings special, you're setting a positive tone that can influence everything that follows.

As you experiment with different ways to infuse your mornings, pay attention to what truly resonates with you. The goal is to create a morning routine that not only prepares you for the day ahead but also brings you joy and fulfillment in the present moment.

But, as you create your personal morning sanctuary, be prepared for inner resistance to creep in. You might hear voices questioning the value of these rituals. Remember, these doubts are normal and can even guide you towards a deeper understanding of what truly matters to you.

With your morning infused with purpose, let's focus on planning your day effectively.

S – STRATEGIZE Your Day

Strategizing isn't just about planning tasks; it's about navigating the maze of possibilities each day presents. You'll face crossroads and decisions. Trust in your ability to choose paths that align with your values and goals.

Strategizing your day means prioritizing your tasks, aligning them with your broader goals, and creating a flexible plan that moves you forward, not just keeps you busy. It's about making deliberate choices that direct your efforts toward meaningful progress rather than getting caught up in the whirlwind of busyness.

Here's How to Set Yourself Up for Success:

1. **Prioritize:** Focus on what's most important. Start by listing all the tasks you need to do, then identify the ones that align closely with your long-term goals.

   Use a prioritization method like the Eisenhower Matrix to categorize tasks into:

   - Urgent and important
   - Important but not urgent
   - Urgent but not important
   - Neither urgent nor important

Concentrate your energy on tasks that are both urgent and important, but don't neglect those that are important but not urgent, because they significantly contribute to your long-term success.

1. **Flexible Schedule:** Have a plan but be ready to adjust. Life happens, and the ability to shift focus as needed is key to staying on track. Create a schedule that outlines your major tasks and goals for the day but leave buffer time for unexpected events or interruptions.
2. **Reflect and Adapt:** At the end of the day, take a few moments to reflect on what you did and what you learned.

   - Did you complete your most important tasks?

- Were there any obstacles that derailed your plans?

Use these insights to adapt and improve your strategy for the next day. Continuous reflection and adjustment help fine-tune your approach, making each day more productive than the last.

Exercise: For one week, end each day by writing down your top three priorities for the next day. In the morning, review these priorities and plan your day around them. At the end of the week, reflect on how this practice affected your productivity and focus.

Reflection: How often do you find yourself working on urgent but unimportant tasks? What strategies could you implement to focus more on important, goal-aligned activities?

Remember, strategizing your day is not just about creating a to-do list; it's about crafting a purposeful and flexible plan that guides you toward meaningful accomplishments. By prioritizing your tasks and keeping a flexible schedule, you set yourself up for a productive and fulfilling day.

As you practice strategizing your day, you'll likely find that you become more adept at distinguishing between what's truly important and what's merely urgent or habitual. This skill is invaluable not just for daily productivity, but for long-term success and satisfaction in both your personal and professional life.

A solid strategy sets the stage. Now, let's put your plan into action.

E – EXECUTE Your Plan

This final phase, EXECUTE, is where your morning preparation meets the day's opportunities and challenges. This phase transforms ideas into action and plans into reality. It's the action that moves you from intention to accomplishment, ensuring the momentum built in the morning carries you through the day with focus, purpose, and satisfaction.

Execution is the bridge between what you envision during your morning ritual and what you achieve by the end of the day. By executing effectively, you turn potential into progress, making sure each step aligns with your goals and is driven by the morning's momentum. You may encounter unexpected obstacles or moments of self-doubt. View these as opportunities to apply the strength and focus you've cultivated in your morning routine.

Here's Your Plan to Get Things Done:

1. **Start With What Matters:** Tackle your biggest or most important task first. This sets the tone for a productive day. Beginning with the most significant task creates a sense of achievement early on. This not only boosts your confidence but also creates positive momentum that propels you through the rest of your tasks.

2. **Stay Focused:** Keep focused and avoid distractions. Remember your priorities and keep working towards them throughout the day. In our distraction-filled world, keeping focus can be challenging but essential.

3. **Celebrate Progress:** Recognize what you've accomplished. It's important to see how your efforts each morning help you achieve your goals. Celebrating progress isn't just about checking off items on a to-do list; it's about acknowledging the effort and steps taken towards your larger goals.

At the end of each task, take a moment to reflect on what you've achieved. This could be as simple as a deep breath and a smile, a brief note in your journal, or sharing your accomplishment with a supportive friend or colleague. Celebrating these small wins keeps you motivated, reinforces positive habits, and provides a sense of closure before moving on to the next task.

Exercise: For one week, use the "eat the frog" technique: identify your most challenging or important task for the day and complete it first thing in the morning. At the end of the week, reflect on how this impacted your productivity and stress levels.

Reflection: How do you typically approach your daily tasks? Do you tend to procrastinate on important but challenging work? How might shifting your most significant task to the beginning of your day change your overall productivity and satisfaction?

As you embark on this journey of morning transformation, you'll likely face obstacles—from the temptation to hit snooze to doubts about the impact of these small changes. But remember, each challenge you overcome strengthens your resolve and brings you closer to your ideal morning routine.

Execution is where your day's plan comes alive. By starting with what matters most, staying focused, and celebrating your progress, you ensure that your actions are purposeful and aligned with your goals. Each task completed isn't just a step forward in your day; it's a step closer to your long-term aspirations.

Remember, effective execution is a skill that improves with practice. As you refine your approach, you'll likely find that you become more efficient and effective in your work. This isn't just about getting more done; it's about achieving what's truly important to you and feeling a sense of accomplishment at the end of each day.

With your morning preparation seamlessly flowing into a day of purposeful action, you'll find that the momentum built through the RISE framework propels you toward a fulfilling and productive life. As you implement the RISE framework, you'll find that mastering your mornings is a journey of self-discovery. Each day presents a new maze to navigate, filled with challenges and opportunities. Your morning routine is your guide through this labyrinth of time.

The Power of Morning Routines

Morning routines aren't just a trend; they're backed by science. Research shows that structured morning rituals can significantly impact our productivity, well-being, and life satisfaction.

1. **Productivity and Mood:** Studies have found that "morning people" often report feeling more proactive and achieve higher job performance ratings. Early risers also tend to report feeling happier and healthier.
2. **Decision-Making and Willpower:** Our ability to make decisions and exercise willpower is often at its peak in the morning. This suggests that important choices are best made during these hours when our mental resources are fresh.
3. **Stress Reduction and Health:** Morning meditation or mindfulness practices have been linked to lower cortisol levels throughout the day, aiding in stress management. Additionally, exposure to morning sunlight has been associated with maintaining a healthy weight.
4. **Habit Formation:** Consistent morning routines can serve as a foundation for building lasting, positive habits. Research suggests it takes about two months for a new behavior to become automatic.

These findings highlight how aligning our daily rituals with our biology can optimize our mornings, setting a positive tone for the entire day and leading to improved performance and increased life satisfaction.

Reflection Questions:

- Which of your current morning habits are most beneficial?
- What new ritual could you introduce to improve your mornings?
- How might your ideal morning routine look different from your current one?

Exercise: Design Your Ideal Morning Take a moment to sketch out your ideal morning routine. Include elements from each phase of RISE. Remember, this is personal. What works for others might not work for you.

As we wrap up this chapter on the RISE Framework, remember that each morning presents a new opportunity for growth, productivity, and joy. By embracing these practices, you're not just optimizing your mornings; you're transforming your entire approach to life. But understanding these concepts is just the beginning. To truly internalize the power of the RISE Framework, we must experience it in a deeper, more visceral way. That's why I invite you now to prepare for an extraordinary journey.

In the pages that follow, you'll find yourself standing at the entrance of a mysterious and profound labyrinth: The Maze of Morning Miracles. This maze is no ordinary construct of hedges or stone; it's a living, breathing manifestation of your inner world, where each turn represents a choice in your morning routine, and each path reflects the consequences of those choices.

As you step into this immersive experience, you'll navigate the twists and turns of setting up a powerful morning ritual. You'll face the whispers of doubt that often derail our best intentions, confront the obstacles that stand between you and your ideal morning, and discover hidden reservoirs of strength you never knew you had.

The Maze of Morning Miracles will challenge you, inspire you, and ultimately transform your understanding of what it means to start your day with purpose and power. It's an adventure that will bring the RISE Framework to life in ways you never imagined.

So, take a deep breath and center yourself. Open your mind to the possibilities that await. What secrets will the maze reveal? What challenges will you overcome? And how will this journey change the way you approach each new day?

Prepare yourself for an exploration that goes beyond mere understanding—an adventure that will etch the principles of RISE into your very being. The Maze of Morning Miracles awaits, ready to guide you towards a profound realization of your potential and the true power of your mornings.

The Maze of Morning Miracles

———

As the last lines of "Rituals of the Rising Sun" linger in your thoughts, you stand up, filled with a sense of purpose. This chapter, introducing you to the RISE framework has not just caught your interest; it has ignited a desire to bring these ideas to life as part of your morning routine. The early morning light fills the room, signaling the fresh start promised by the day.

A new day dawns, brimming with potential.

Feeling motivated by what you've learned and the chance for self-improvement, you begin to integrate the RISE principles into your morning. 'Revitalize' encourages you to start with some light stretching, movements that mirror the waking world outside. Each stretch, each deep breath, is a step towards aligning your body and mind, preparing them for the day's challenges.

The whispers of doubt creep in.

However, as you take a moment to 'Infuse' your morning with prayer and reflection, hoping to set a positive tone for the day, a shadow of doubt creeps in. Instead of one voice, you hear many, questioning:

- "Is this short moment really going to impact your whole day, or is it just a tiny action against a backdrop of chaos?"
- "Can this reflection make a difference against the pile of tasks awaiting you?"
- "Do these prayers actually fortify you, or are they merely quiet words drowned out by the day's demands?"

Determination rises to meet the challenge.

Facing these questions, you find not discouragement but motivation. Each doubt strengthens your resolve, sharpening your focus on what you set out to achieve. You see these questions not as signs of failure but as hurdles to clear on your path to success.

Your inner voice speaks truth.

"Every prayer," you remind yourself, "lays the foundation for the day, serving as a clear moment amidst life's storms. It's not just a minor detail; it's the wave that can change everything."

You find a powerful balance between thinking deeply and taking action. You tell yourself, "A moment of prayer and reflection is more powerful than a long to-do list, because it roots me in my purpose, turning every task into a meaningful step forward."

Inner strength becomes your anchor.

Facing doubts about your inner strength, you respond with confidence, "My moments of prayer and reflection are the solid ground I stand on. They are not just fleeting thoughts but the core of my strength, helping me face daily challenges with faith and focus."

Reality shifts, and the adventure begins.

Suddenly, the room you knew transforms into an expansive maze. Towering walls and mist-covered paths mark this as no ordinary labyrinth but a maze of time, brimming with moments both seized and missed, beckoning you to embark on an exploration through the rich tapestry of life.

You step into the unknown.

Feeling both lost and intrigued, you rise and step into the Maze of Moments. The air is alive with echoes of the past and whispers of the future, intertwining in the gentle breeze. Here, every step is more than mere movement; it's a voyage through the moments that compose our existence.

The maze mirrors life's complexities.

As you navigate through the maze, each turn and path present a new challenge. You come across narrow corridors that represent the constraints of time, and wide-open spaces that symbolize opportunities. You see paths that loop back on themselves, reminding you of the cyclical nature of some tasks and habits. The walls of the maze are adorned with murals that depict various phases of life—moments of joy, sorrow, success, and failure.

How do you feel when faced with these visual representations of life's journey?

- Do you feel overwhelmed by the complexity of the path ahead?
- Are you excited by the potential for growth and discovery?

A profound realization dawns.

The realization hits gently yet with profound impact: you are the labyrinth itself. Every twist, turn, and obstacle reflects the trials of weaving the RISE routine into your life. More crucially, they are the vast opportunities for growth and transformation inherent in these challenges.

Your inner dialogue transforms.

The doubts you had about your impact weren't setbacks. Instead, they pushed you to look deeper into yourself. These doubts challenged you to examine how committed and determined you really are.

The maze becomes a guide.

With this deeper understanding, the once daunting maze walls transform into guides on your path to self-betterment. What seemed confusing before is now clear.

Your choices help you:

R - Revitalize your mind, body, and spirit

I - Infuse good morning practices

S - Strategize effectively

E - Execute consistently

Your journey becomes meaningful exploration.

Through this new lens, the maze shifts from a perplexing puzzle to a meaningful exploration of self. It changes from a confusing mess to a clear path of self-discovery. Each step moves you forward and closer to your goals. This shows the power of starting each day with purpose.

Calm settles as wisdom is gained.

As you weave through the maze's final curves, a calm covers you. The labyrinth, once a metaphor for inner turmoil and uncertainty, now symbolizes your evolution and fortitude. You acknowledge that each new day presents its own labyrinth of choices and hurdles. However, armed with the wisdom gained from today's adventure, you face them not as obstacles but as avenues for further discovery.

Transformation complete, you rise renewed.

Leaving the Maze of Morning Miracles, you gain more than just success. You now have a guide for living each day with purpose and focus. The RISE framework becomes more than a to-do list. It's now a powerful way to care for your whole self - body, mind, and spirit.

A bridge from thought to action forms.

This insight, sparked within the labyrinth, forms a bridge from thought to action, from simply existing to fully living. It's constructed from moments of doubt and triumph, creating a path illuminated by the understanding that every day is a journey, every challenge a lesson, and every instant an opportunity to see your own growth.

What key lessons will you carry forward from this journey through the Maze of Morning Miracles?

- How has your perception of morning routines changed?
- What new commitment will you make to your daily rituals?

The adventure ends, but your journey continues.

As you step back into your familiar surroundings, you feel a profound shift in your perspective. The RISE framework is no longer just a concept but a living, breathing part of your approach to each day. You're filled with anticipation for the dawn, eager to put into practice the insights gained from your journey through the Maze of Morning Miracles.

As you prepare for sleep, you set your intention for tomorrow, knowing that each sunrise brings a new opportunity to navigate life's maze with purpose, awareness, and the transformative power of a well-crafted morning routine.

THE FOCUS FRONTIER

"In the currency of attention, focus is the investment that yields the greatest returns."

With your new understanding of time, you are now at a crucial point. It's time to move from thinking to action, considering your next steps. Coming up, the Forest of Focused Fortitude will put your newfound understanding to the test. As you navigate its winding paths and face its unique obstacles, you'll gain profound insights into the true value of your time.

For now, as we step into the realm of THE FOCUS FRONTIER, we're diving deeper into the heart of our journey towards mastering focus and productivity. You've already laid the groundwork, understanding the principles that set the stage for a transformative way of working and living. Now, it's time to build on that foundation with the FOCUS Framework, a structured approach designed to take your productivity and engagement to the next level.

Remember the insights gained from your journey through the Maze of Morning Miracles. Just as you navigated those twists and turns, you'll now face the challenge of keeping focus amidst life's distractions.

How will your morning routine support your focus throughout the day?

This framework isn't merely about following steps; it's a comprehensive method that reshapes how you approach your daily tasks, projects, and overarching goals. More than boosting productivity, it's about nurturing a mindset and an environment conducive to deep, meaningful work that resonates with your core values and drives.

In this chapter, we'll dissect the FOCUS Framework, piece by piece, revealing how each element can transform your ability to achieve and sustain those moments of flow — those periods where everything just clicks, and you're completely absorbed in your work. But achieving flow is about more than dodging distractions or ticking off a to-do list. It's about crafting a life where your work harmonizes with your passions, guiding you ever closer to realizing your fullest potential.

Reflection: How has your perspective on time changed since beginning this journey?

Now that we've set the stage, let's dive into what truly drives productivity.

The Essence of True Productivity

True productivity isn't just about ticking off tasks on your to-do list or filling every moment with activity. It's about ensuring that your actions align with what genuinely matters to you; your big goals, your dreams, and what makes you feel fulfilled at the end of the day.

Exercise: List three activities that make you feel truly productive. What do these activities have in common?

With this understanding, let's explore a framework designed to maximize your focus and productivity.

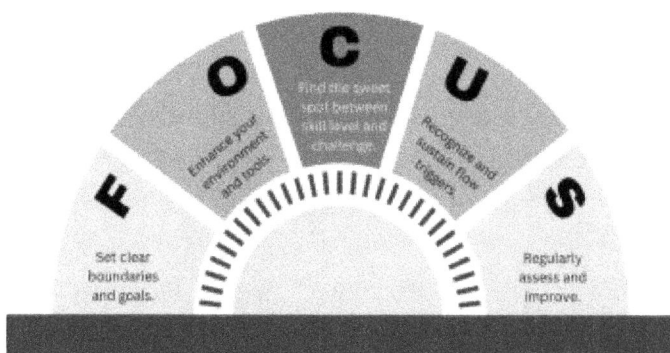

The FOCUS Framework:

To help you achieve peak productivity, let's introduce the FOCUS Framework:

1. **F**rame your mind and environment
2. **O**ptimize for intrinsic motivation
3. **C**hallenge-skill balance
4. **U**nderstanding flow
5. **S**elf-reflect and grow

Now let's break down each part of the FOCUS Framework:

F – FRAME Your Mind

First things first: let's focus on framing—preparing your mind and your workspace for peak productivity. This step is about creating an environment and a mindset that are perfectly tuned for deep work. It's like setting the stage for a performance where you're the star, ready to give your best show.

By honing your surroundings and your mental focus, you set yourself up for those moments of flow, where you and your work are in perfect harmony. Think about your ideal workspace. What does it look like? How does it feel? Now, consider how you can bring elements of that ideal into your current environment.

Practical Tips:

- Choose a specific area for focused work
- Remove potential distractions before starting
- Use rituals to signal your brain it's time to focus

Consider how your morning routine, set up through the RISE framework, can set the stage for focused work. How can you carry that intentionality into your focus sessions?

What obstacles might you encounter in maintaining this focus, and how will you overcome them?

Exercise: Take a moment to assess your current workspace. Write down three changes you can make right now to create a more conducive environment for focus.

NOTE: This could be as simple as clearing clutter, adjusting lighting, or creating a dedicated work area.

With your environment set, let's fuel your work with genuine motivation.

O – OPTIMIZE for Intrinsic Motivation

Next, let's talk about fueling your work with genuine passion and purpose. Optimizing for intrinsic motivation is about aligning your tasks with your personal values and long-term goals. When your work resonates with what truly matters to you, productivity becomes less about forcing yourself to stay on task, and more about flowing naturally from one meaningful activity to the next.

Consider the tasks on your to-do list. How do they connect to your broader life goals or personal values? Finding these connections can transform even mundane tasks into steppingstones towards your larger aspirations.

Reflect on the moments of clarity you experienced in the Maze of Morning Miracles. How can you tap into that same sense of purpose and motivation in your daily tasks?

Values Alignment Exercise List your top 5 personal values. For each task on your to-do list, rate how well it aligns with these values on a scale of 1-10. Prioritize tasks that score higher and find ways to connect lower-scoring tasks to your values.

The Neuroscience of Motivation Understanding the brain's reward system can boost motivation. When we accomplish tasks aligned with our values, our brain releases dopamine, reinforcing the behavior. By consciously connecting our work to our values, we can create a positive feedback loop of motivation and achievement. With motivation in place, it's time to balance challenge and skill for optimal engagement.

C – CHALLENGE-SKILL Balance

The sweet spot for productivity and engagement lies in the balance between the challenge of a task and your skill level. Tasks that are too easy lead to boredom, while those that are too difficult can cause anxiety. The goal is to find the "Goldilocks Zone" where you're stretched just enough to grow and stay engaged, but not so much that you feel overwhelmed.

This balance isn't static; as your skills improve, you'll need to seek out greater challenges to keep that optimal state of flow and productivity.

Practical Applications:

1. **For routine tasks:** For example, if your usual workout is getting too easy, challenge yourself to increase the weight, reps, or introduce new exercises.
2. **For complex projects:** Break them down into smaller, manageable steps. Start with tasks that are well within your comfort zone to build momentum, then gradually move to more challenging aspects as your confidence and skill grow.
3. **For skill development:** Use the "Plus One" technique. Always aim to perform at a level slightly above your current ability.

As you prepare to navigate the Forest of Focused Fortitude, consider how you'll apply this balance principle. Each challenge you face will test your ability to match your skills with the task at hand.

What hidden strengths will you discover as you face these challenges?

Deliberate Practice: To keep the right challenge-skill balance, engage in deliberate practice.

This involves:

1. Setting specific goals for improvement
2. Seeking immediate feedback
3. Focusing intently on areas of weakness
4. Consistently pushing slightly beyond your current abilities

This approach ensures you're always in that productive "stretch zone" and sets the stage for achieving a state of flow.

U – UNDERSTAND Flow

Flow is the pinnacle of productivity—a state where you're so deeply absorbed in a task that time seems to evaporate. It's more than just feeling good; it's about reaching your peak performance. In flow, your creativity soars, efficiency skyrockets, and satisfaction with your work deepens.

Achieving flow isn't about luck or chance. It's a skill you can cultivate by recognizing and recreating the conditions that trigger this state for you. Maybe it's the quiet of early morning, the buzz of a busy café, or the challenge of a complex problem. Whatever your triggers, identifying them is the first step to harnessing the power of flow.

Understanding flow isn't just about chasing a fleeting feeling, it's about consistently tapping into your highest potential. As you become more adept at entering flow states, you'll find that not only does your productivity increase, but your overall enjoyment of work is amplified. This is where productivity transcends mere output and becomes a deeply satisfying expression of your capabilities.

Strategies for Entering Flow:

1. **Clear Goals:** Set specific, challenging but achievable goals for your work session.
2. **Immediate Feedback:** Create systems that provide quick

feedback on your progress.

3. **Distraction-Free Environment:** Drop potential interruptions before starting.
4. **Matched Challenge-Skill Level:** Choose tasks that stretch your abilities without overwhelming you.
5. **Deep Focus:** Use techniques like the Pomodoro method to keep concentrated effort.

The Forest of Focused Fortitude will present numerous opportunities to experience and understand flow. Pay attention to the moments when you feel fully immersed in a task, losing track of time and self-consciousness. These are the states you'll aim to recreate in your daily work.

Overcoming Obstacles to Flow:

1. **External Distractions:** Use noise-cancelling headphones, "do not disturb" signs, or dedicated workspaces.
2. **Internal Distractions:** Practice mindfulness to manage wandering thoughts.
3. **Lack of Clear Goals:** Break larger projects into specific, actionable tasks.
4. **Skill-Challenge Mismatch:** Adjust tasks to better align with your current skill level.
5. **Low Energy:** Schedule challenging tasks during your peak energy hours.

Technology and Flow While technology can be a distraction, it can also help flow when used mindfully. Consider using goal-tracking apps to stay motivated and monitor your progress. Additionally, binaural beats can create a sound environment that enhances focus and flow.

Measuring Flow Keep a "flow journal." After work sessions, rate your flow state on a scale of 1-10 and note the conditions present. Over time, you'll identify patterns that help you enter flow more consistently.

Understanding flow leads us to our final, crucial step: reflection and growth.

S – SELF-REFLECT and Grow

This final piece of the FOCUS Framework is perhaps the most crucial for long-term success. Regular self-reflection allows you to continuously refine your approach, learning from both your successes and your setbacks.

This isn't about harsh self-criticism, but rather a compassionate, curious examination of your work habits and their outcomes. By understanding what works best for you, you can steadily improve your focus and productivity over time.

Structured Reflection Template:

Daily Reflection (5 minutes):

1. What was my most productive period today, and why?
2. Did I experience any moments of flow? What contributed to them?
3. What's one thing I can do tomorrow to improve my focus?

Weekly Reflection (15 minutes):

1. What were my biggest accomplishments this week?
2. Which tasks or activities drained my energy the most?
3. How well did I maintain my focus routines?
4. What new strategy can I implement next week to enhance my productivity?

By consistently engaging in this practice, you'll gain invaluable insights into your work patterns and how to optimize them. While our framework provides a strong foundation, let's address a common enemy of focus: distractions.

Dealing with Distractions:

In our hyper-connected world, distractions are abundant and can significantly impede our ability to focus. Understanding the nature of these distractions and developing strategies to manage them is crucial for maintaining productivity.

Types of Distractions:

1. **External Distractions:** Noise, notifications, interruptions from colleagues.
2. **Internal Distractions:** Wandering thoughts, anxiety, hunger.
3. **Digital Distractions:** Social media, emails, unnecessary web browsing.

Strategies for Managing Distractions:

1. **Environment Control:** Create a dedicated workspace that minimizes external distractions.
2. **Digital Detox:** Use website blockers and app limits to control digital distractions.
3. **Mindfulness Practices:** Regular meditation can improve your ability to notice and dismiss distracting thoughts.
4. **Time-Blocking:** Allocate specific times for potentially distracting activities like checking emails.
5. **The Two-Minute Rule:** If a task takes less than two minutes, do it immediately to prevent it from becoming a lingering distraction.

Beyond managing distractions, cultivating the right mindset is key to sustained productivity.

Cultivating a Productivity Mindset:

Productivity is as much about mindset as it is about tactics. Cultivate these attitudes to enhance your focus and efficiency:

1. **Growth Mindset:** View challenges as opportunities to learn and improve.

   - **Practice:** When facing a challenging task, ask yourself, "What can I learn from this?"

1. **Patience:** Understand that meaningful progress takes time.

   - Practice: Set both short-term and long-term goals to appreciate incremental progress.

1. **Flexibility:** Be willing to adjust your approach when needed.

   - **Practice:** Regularly review and adjust your productivity strategies based on what's working and what isn't.

1. **Resilience:** Bounce back from setbacks and view them as learning opportunities.

   - **Practice:** After a setback, list three lessons learned and how you'll apply them moving forward.

1. **Curiosity:** Keep an inquisitive attitude towards your work and processes.

   - **Practice:** Ask "Why?" and "How can this be improved?"

about your tasks and methods.

Exercise: Mindset Reflection At the end of each week, reflect on how these mindsets influenced your productivity. Note specific instances where you exhibited (or struggled with) each mindset and the resulting impact on your work.

By consistently engaging in this practice, you'll gain invaluable insights into your work patterns and how to optimize them. Armed with these tools and mindsets, you're ready to put them into practice.

Cultivating a Productivity Mindset

Productivity is as much about mindset as it is about tactics. Cultivate these attitudes:

1. **Growth mindset:** View challenges as opportunities to learn and improve
2. **Patience:** Understand that meaningful progress takes time
3. **Flexibility:** Be willing to adjust your approach when needed

Your Productivity Journey

Remember, the FOCUS Framework is flexible. If you're a night owl, your "Frame" period might be in the evening. If you thrive on variety, rotate your focus techniques. The key is consistency in application, not rigid adherence to a one-size-fits-all approach.

Armed with the FOCUS Framework, take a moment to reflect on how these newfound strategies have sharpened your mental acuity. The power to direct your attention with precision is now at your fingertips, ready to transform how you approach both challenges and opportunities.

With your mind primed for concentration, you turn to your inbox, ready to tackle the afternoon's tasks. Suddenly, an unexpected email catches your eye, as if responding to your heightened state of focus...

The Forest of Focused Fortitude

———

As you skim through your usual emails, one subject line stands out, drawing you in with its intrigue: "Begin Your Time Mastery Journey: A New Chapter Awaits." It sparks curiosity and a hint of excitement.

You can't help but click on it.

> *Dear Explorer of Time,*
>
> *Today isn't just another set of hours passing by; it marks the beginning of a profound journey towards mastering yourself. This message opens the door to controlling how you spend your days and unlock your true potential...*

Your thoughts start to wander. The phrase "unlock your true potential" from the email echoes inside your head. As it does, your surroundings begin to blur, reality shifting and focusing inward on a deep, vivid journey within yourself.

Then, everything shifts in a heartbeat.

Suddenly, you're standing at the entrance of a grand maze. Ancient stones tower around you, whispering tales of the past and hinting at the mysteries of time itself. The air is electric, charged with anticipation for what lies ahead.

Your morning routine becomes your strength.

As you enter the Forest of Focused Fortitude, you feel energized from your morning routine. Your earlier efforts make you more alert here. You see how your morning habits have prepared you for this challenge, giving you a clear mind and sense of purpose to face what's ahead.

A mysterious voice sets the challenge.

A voice echoes through the forest: "Welcome to the Forest of Focused Fortitude. Here, you'll learn to set priorities and plan effectively. Your challenge is to navigate this maze before the sand in your hourglass runs out.

Each path represents a task or decision. Choose wisely - some paths may seem urgent but might not lead you to your goal. Remember, the shortest route isn't always the best. Use your time management skills to make the right choices and find the exit."

Time becomes tangible in your hands.

As you grip the hourglass, you feel its weight - a tangible reminder of your limited time. The maze stretches before you, its twisting paths representing the many choices you face each day. Some paths beckon with urgency, while others, though less pressing, might be more important.

Your journey of focus begins.

With determination, you take your first step into the maze, ready to put your focus and decision-making skills to the test.

FRAMING Your Mind

Before long, you're facing a choice. To your left, a path shouts for attention, marked 'Urgent!' To your right, a more subdued trail, marked 'Important,' waits patiently. While trying to decide which path to take, you hear whispers of self-doubt:

"You'll never get through this maze in time.

Why even try?" "Look at all these paths - you'll definitely choose the wrong one."

"You're not cut out for this. Maybe you should just give up now."

These voices mirror the internal struggles you face daily when trying to focus and make decisions. The weight of these thoughts feels as tangible as the stone walls surrounding you.

A moment of clarity breaks through.

Surrounded by these whispers of doubt, you pause, taking a deep breath. You recall the strategies you've learned for managing these overwhelming thoughts. "These are just thoughts," you remind yourself, "not facts." As you center yourself, the whispers begin to fade, not disappearing entirely, but losing their grip on your resolve.

Wisdom guides your choice.

With a clearer mind, you face the choice before you. The 'Urgent' path beckons loudly, its call of immediate action almost irresistible. For a moment, you feel the familiar pull of reactivity, the urge to rush and tackle whatever seems most pressing.

But then you remember the lessons on prioritizing what really matters. You realize that importance often whispers while urgency shouts. With this insight, you make your choice. Deliberately, you opt for the path less traveled, marked 'Important,' favoring enduring significance over fleeting urgency.

Your morning routine proves its worth.

As you commit to the 'Important' path, you notice how your decision mirrors the intentionality of your morning routine. The clarity you gained earlier helps you resist the loud calls of urgency, allowing you to maintain focus on what truly matters. You realize that the mental frame you set in the morning is now supporting your ability to make wise choices in the face of distraction.

Uncertainty and determination intertwine.

As you step onto this path, you feel a mix of uncertainty and determination. It may not provide the immediate satisfaction of tackling urgent tasks, but deep down, you know this choice aligns more closely with your true goals and values.

How do you feel when choosing between urgency and importance?

- Do you feel overwhelmed by the pressure of immediate tasks?
- Do you feel relieved when focusing on long-term goals?

A new challenge awaits.

Standing before the chamber with four doors, you recall the sense of purpose you felt during your morning reflection. That same feeling resurfaces now, helping you connect with your deeper motivations. You realize that the moments of clarity you experienced earlier have prepared you to align your choices here with your true values and long-term goals.

OPTIMIZING for Intrinsic Motivation

As you venture deeper into the Forest of Focused Fortitude, the path opens into a circular clearing. At its center stands an ancient stone chamber, its weathered surface etched with mysterious symbols. Four ornate doors dominate its facade, each radiating a different energy that seems to pull at your consciousness.

You recall the sense of purpose you felt during your morning reflection, and that same feeling resurfaces now, helping you connect with your deeper motivations. The clarity you gained earlier has prepared you to face this new challenge.

As you approach, you realize each door represents a quadrant of the Eisenhower Matrix, a powerful tool for prioritization you learned about in the FOCUS Framework:

- **Urgent and Important:** A door of blazing red, humming with intensity
- **Important but Not Urgent:** A door of deep blue, exuding a calm yet powerful presence
- **Urgent but Not Important:** A door of flickering yellow, its energy frantic and distracting
- **Neither Urgent nor Important:** A door of muted gray, almost fading into the background

A chamber of choice materializes before you.

You stand at the threshold of decision, feeling the weight of choice. Each door seems to whisper promises and warnings. You know that your choice will not only determine your path through the forest but also reflect your ability to align your actions with your true values and long-term goals.

Intrinsic motivation becomes your compass.

As you contemplate your options, you remember the lessons on intrinsic motivation. You ask yourself, "Which of these paths truly resonates with my deepest aspirations? How can I use this moment to reinforce my commitment to what genuinely matters?"

The forest holds its breath, awaiting your decision.

The forest around you seems to hold its breath, waiting for your decision. You realize that this chamber is more than just a test—it's an opportunity to put your newfound skills into practice, to demonstrate your understanding of prioritization and your commitment to meaningful progress.

You stand at the crossroads of urgency and importance.

With a deep breath, you step forward, ready to make your choice...

As you consider the 'Urgent' and 'Important' paths, anxiety creeps in. The 'Urgent' path calls loudly, playing on your fears of falling behind or missing out. It's tempting to rush down this familiar route of immediate gratification. The 'Important' path, though quieter, resonates with a deeper part of you, but choosing it means facing the discomfort of delayed reward.

Your heart races as the moment of truth arrives.

You stand at this crossroads, feeling the pull of both paths. Your heart races as you weigh the options, the pressure of making the right choice bearing down on you. You close your eyes, taking a deep breath to center yourself.

A moment of clarity illuminates your path.

In this moment of stillness, you recall the Eisenhower Matrix you learned about. You visualize its four quadrants, each representing a different type of task: Urgent and Important, Important but Not Urgent, Urgent but Not Important, and Neither Urgent nor Important.

This mental image helps calm your racing thoughts. You realize that this choice isn't just about now, but about shaping your future path. With renewed clarity, you step forward, ready to face each decision point with this framework in mind.

As you move through the maze, you encounter doors representing each quadrant of the matrix. Each choice feels weighty, but you approach them with a newfound sense of purpose. You find yourself naturally gravitating towards the tasks that align with your long-term goals and values, even when they don't demand immediate attention.

Empowerment grows with each deliberate choice.

Navigating through these doors, your decisions highlight your truest priorities, unveiling the strength of deliberate decision-making. You begin to feel a sense of empowerment, recognizing that each choice is a step towards the life you genuinely want to lead.

CHALLENGING Your Skill

In the heart of the forest, you find yourself in a clearing surrounded by towering walls that seem to touch the sky. The once-familiar path has transformed into an intricate maze of stone and vegetation. As the sun begins to set, casting long shadows across the ground, doubt creeps in, subtly altering your perception. What appeared manageable now looms insurmountable, much like how twilight can turn familiar landscapes into mysterious terrains.

Excitement and apprehension intertwine.

You feel a mix of excitement and apprehension coursing through you. This, you realize, is the perfect opportunity to apply the challenge-skill balance principle from the FOCUS Framework. You take a deep breath, centering yourself and recalling the strengths you've discovered on your journey so far.

As you begin to navigate the obstacles, you draw on abilities you didn't know you possessed. Your fingers find minute cracks in the seemingly smooth walls, your feet discover hidden footholds in the twisting vines. With each small victory, your confidence grows, revealing new facets of your capabilities.

Doubt whispers as you face a crucial decision.

Am I making wise choices?

The question echoes in your mind as you pause at a fork in the maze. The path to the left looks easier but longer, while the right appears treacherous but more direct. You remember that true growth often lies just beyond your comfort zone.

Complexity grows as night approaches.

Can I sort through this complex web of decisions?

You wonder, as the maze seems to shift and change with the fading light. What seemed simple in broad daylight now grows increasingly complex, mirroring how the approaching night can transform the familiar into the unknown.

Each challenge becomes a steppingstone to growth.

Yet, with each challenge you overcome, you feel a surge of accomplishment. You're stretching your skills to match the difficulty of the task at hand, finding that sweet spot where growth occurs. As you scale a particularly daunting wall, you can't help but wonder, "What other hidden strengths might I discover in this forest?"

The journey transforms you with each step.

The maze continues to test you, presenting a series of escalating challenges. Sometimes you stumble, but each setback teaches you something new about your capabilities and resilience. You realize that this journey isn't just about reaching the end of the maze—it's about becoming a more skilled, confident version of yourself.

Your senses sharpen as you adapt to the unknown.

You find that your other senses have sharpened to compensate for the lack of visibility. The forest has indeed turned the well-known into something uncertain, but you're adapting, growing, rising to meet each new challenge with newfound strength and determination.

UNDERSTANDING Your Flow

As you progress deeper into the forest, you encounter a series of intricate gates, each demanding a portion of your time and presenting unique challenges. The complexity of the situation strikes you, mirroring the multifaceted nature of daily life.

Doubt whispers in the face of complexity.

How should I divide my time? What if I make the wrong choice?

These questions echo in your mind, reflecting the constant struggle of prioritization.

As you contemplate your options, you recall the flow concept from the FOCUS Framework. You take a deep breath, centering yourself, and decide to approach each gate with full presence and intention.

Time bends as you enter a state of flow.

You begin with the first gate, focusing all your attention on the task at hand. As you engage with the challenge, something remarkable happens. Time seems to slow, your actions become fluid and effortless, and your self-consciousness fades away. You recognize this state – it's flow, just as described in the framework.

Confidence grows with each challenge conquered.

Energized by this realization, you move from gate to gate with growing confidence. Each challenge, while unique, becomes an opportunity to enter this state of peak performance. You notice how your morning routine has prepared you for this, providing a foundation of mindfulness that supports your ability to achieve flow.

The forest tests your resolve.

However, as you press on, the forest seems to stretch endlessly before you. The gates become more complex. The challenges become more daunting. Shadows deepen with each step, and your initial confidence begins to waver. The thrill of the flow state becomes harder to achieve, leaving you questioning your choices.

Fatigue sets in as you navigate this intricate path. The initial excitement wears off, replaced by a gnawing sense of overwhelm. "Is this even worth it?" you wonder, feeling the pull of distraction and the desire to give up.

A glimmer of hope reignites your determination.

Just as despair threatens to overtake you, a soft glow catches your eye. It's faint at first, but as you move towards it, the light grows stronger. This gentle illumination seems to whisper encouragement, reminding you of how far you've come.

Renewed strength carries you forward.

With renewed energy, you push forward, tapping into the flow state once again. Each step becomes a little easier, the path a little clearer. You realize that the challenges you've faced haven't weakened you – they've made you stronger, more resilient, and more capable of achieving flow even in difficult circumstances.

The journey's end reveals a transformed you.

As you round the final corner, the forest opens into a serene clearing bathed in warm light. You've reached the final stage of your journey through the Forest of Focused Fortitude. In this tranquil space, you're enveloped in a sense of accomplishment and clarity.

Looking back, you see how each gate, each decision, each moment of doubt, and each experience of flow has contributed to your growth. You've not only navigated the forest but also gained a deeper understanding of your ability to focus, achieve flow, and persevere through challenges.

Take a moment to reflect on your journey. How has your understanding of flow deepened? How can you apply these insights to achieve more flow states in your daily life and work?

As you ponder these questions, a sense of calm washes over you. You realize that this journey wasn't just about reaching the end – it's about the wisdom you've gained along the way. You've experienced firsthand how your morning routine supports your focus throughout the day, how to overcome obstacles by matching your skills to each challenge, and the power of intrinsic motivation and flow.

This is the essence of self-reflection – the ability to look back on your experiences, learn from them, and use those insights to grow stronger and more focused. As you sit in this peaceful clearing, you feel a deep sense of gratitude for the journey and excitement for what lies ahead.

Remember, the skills you've developed in this forest – achieving flow, prioritization, decision-making, and perseverance – are tools you can always carry with you. These skills will serve you well as you continue to navigate the complexities of life and work, helping you to create more flow states and maintain focus even in challenging situations.

SELF-REFLECTING for Growth

At last, you pass through the final gate, and the maze's walls gently disappear, revealing the serene Garden of Achieved Goals. In this tranquil space, you're enveloped in a sense of triumph. The maze, with its many turns and decisions, reflected life's complexities, mirroring the choices we face daily.

Your journey's fruits bloom before you.

As you take in the beauty of this garden, you see that every petal and leaf embodies a victory over adversity and a moment of clarity in decision-making. The air is filled with a sense of accomplishment, yet it also carries the promise of future growth.

Reflection becomes your tool for growth.

You find a comfortable spot to sit and reflect on your journey. The struggles you faced in the maze – the self-doubt, the overwhelming choices, the fatigue – all seem to have faded, leaving behind valuable lessons and newfound strength.

What emotions arise when you see the results of your efforts?

- Do you feel satisfaction from achieving goals?

- Do you feel motivation to continue making deliberate choices?

Your insights become a roadmap for the future.

As you ponder these questions, you notice a small journal and pen beside you. Opening it, you see blank pages waiting to be filled with your insights. You begin to write, capturing the key moments of your journey:

1. The initial overwhelm you experienced, and how you overcame it
2. The choice between urgent and important paths
3. How you navigated complex decisions using the Eisenhower Matrix
4. The moment you almost gave up, and what kept you going
5. The final push that led you to this garden

With each word you write, you feel a growing sense of clarity and purpose. You realize that this journey through the Forest of Focused Fortitude wasn't just about reaching a destination – it was about becoming someone new along the way.

A renewed sense of determination propels you forward.

As you close the journal, you feel a renewed sense of energy and determination. The challenges you faced have honed your focus, sharpened your decision-making skills, and strengthened your resolve. You're no longer the same person who entered the forest – you've grown, adapted, and evolved.

New horizons beckon as your journey continues.

Looking ahead, you see a path leading out of the garden, towards new horizons. You know that life will present more mazes, more challenges, but now you have the tools and the confidence to navigate them.

A promise to yourself seals your transformation.

With a deep breath, you stand, ready to leave the Forest of Focused Fortitude behind. As you do, you make a silent promise to yourself: to carry these lessons with you, to continue reflecting and growing, and to approach each new challenge as an opportunity for further mastery of your time and focus.

Your journey of growth continues beyond the forest.

The adventure may be ending, but your journey of growth and self-improvement is just beginning. With each step forward, you're not just managing your time – you're cultivating a mindset primed for success.

A new chapter awaits, promising further transformation.

As you leave the forest behind, you're ready to tackle the next chapter: "MOTIVATE YOUR MINDSET." The lessons you've learned here about focus and decision-making have laid a solid foundation. Now, it's time to supercharge your motivation and transform your mindset into an unstoppable force.

The path ahead promises to reveal the MOTIVATE framework – a toolkit for building a resilient, adaptable, and energized mindset. You feel a surge of excitement, knowing that you're about to learn how to turn every trial into a triumph and every setback into a setup for a comeback.

With renewed determination, you step forward, eager to explore how you can map out your journey, set clear objectives, and create time-bound commitments that will propel you towards your goals. The Forest of Focused Fortitude was just the beginning – now, it's time to unleash the full power of your motivated mindset.

MOTIVATE YOUR MINDSET

———

"Your mindset is the engine of your motivation. Fuel it with positivity, resilience, and unwavering belief in your ability to overcome any obstacle."

Have you ever felt like you're running on a treadmill, expending energy but not really getting anywhere? You've set your goals, established your routines, and even found moments of laser-like focus. But sometimes, life throws a curveball that sends all your carefully laid plans into disarray.

What's missing?

The engine that powers it all: Your Mindset.

In this chapter, we're going to supercharge your motivation by harnessing the power of your mental and emotional state. Tony Robbins, a master of personal development, often speaks about the concept of "state" - the mental and emotional condition you're in at any given moment. Your state directly influences your performance, decisions, and overall quality of life.

But here's the crucial question: Can you learn to control your state, to summon motivation and focus at will?

What techniques will you discover to master your state?

Enter the MOTIVATE framework - your toolkit for building a resilient, adaptable, and energized state of mind. This isn't just another set of tips; it's a comprehensive system designed to help you take control of your mental and emotional state, skyrocketing your motivation and productivity.

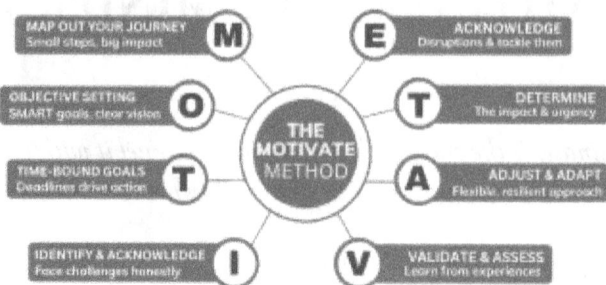

| MAP OUT YOUR JOURNEY | | | | ACKNOWLEDGE |
| Small steps, big impact | (M) | (E) | | Disruptions & tackle them |

The MOTIVATE Framework:

To help you cultivate a resilient, adaptable, and energized mindset, let's introduce the MOTIVATE Framework:

1. **M**ap out small steps
2. **O**bjective setting
3. **T**ime-bound commitments
4. **I**dentify and acknowledge
5. **V**alidate and assess
6. **A**djust and adapt
7. **T**ake Action and evaluate
8. **E**nergize with inspiration

By mastering these elements, you'll develop the ability to shift your state intentionally, maintaining high levels of motivation even in the face of challenges. You'll learn to tap into peak states of performance, turning what once felt like a daily grind into an exciting journey of growth and achievement.

As we dive deeper into the MOTIVATE framework, consider: How will the ability to control your state transform your daily life and long-term success?

What areas of your life will flourish as you master the art of state management?)

Are you ready to unlock the full power of your mindset and motivation?

Let's break down each part of the MOTIVATE Framework:

Each element of MOTIVATE is a powerful tool on its own, but together, they form an unstoppable strategy for tackling challenges, staying motivated, and achieving your wildest dreams.

M - MAP Out Small Steps

Picture this: You're standing at the base of a mountain, your goal glimmering at the distant peak. It's breathtaking, inspiring... and more than a little overwhelming.

But here's a secret: no one climbs a mountain in a single bound. Every epic journey begins with a single step.

That's the power of mapping out small steps. It's about transforming that mountain of a goal into a series of manageable molehills.

Here's why it works:

1. **Manageable Tasks:** Breaking big challenges into smaller parts reduces overwhelm.
2. **Clear Path:** Visualizing your journey helps guide your progress.
3. **Motivation Boost:** Completing small tasks releases dopamine, encouraging further action.

Mastering Your State: As you break down your goal into smaller steps, pay attention to how your emotional state shifts. You'll likely notice a change from feeling overwhelmed to feeling empowered.

This is the power of managing your state through action. Each small step you map out is not just a task to complete, but an opportunity to cultivate a positive, motivated state of mind. As Tony Robbins often says, "Motion creates emotion." By planning and taking these small steps, you're not just making progress towards your goal – you're actively shaping your mental and emotional state, priming yourself for success.

How did the process of mapping out small steps change your emotional state?

Did you feel a shift in your motivation or confidence?

Let's put this into action with a powerful exercise.

Exercise: Goal Breakdown

1. Choose a goal that feels overwhelming. Maybe it's writing a book, launching a business, or learning a new language.
2. Grab a stack of sticky notes and a pen.
3. Start breaking down your goal into the smallest possible steps. Write each step on a separate sticky note.
4. Arrange your sticky notes in order, creating a visual roadmap of your journey.
5. As you complete each step, move its sticky note to a "Done" section. Watch your progress grow!

Reflection Questions:

- How did breaking down your goal make it feel more manageable?

- What emotions did you experience as you created your roadmap?
- How can you apply this technique to other areas of your life?

Remember, every great achievement in history started with a single step. By mapping out your small steps, you're not just planning - you're paving your path to success. So, what's your first step going to be?

O - OBJECTIVE Setting

Now that we've broken down our mountain into manageable molehills, it's time to get crystal clear on what we're aiming for. Objective setting is like calibrating your GPS before a long journey - without it, you might be moving, but are you really getting anywhere?

The Power of Clear Goals

Imagine trying to hit a target while blindfolded. Pretty tough, right? That's what trying to achieve success without clear objectives feels like. When you set clear, specific goals, you're taking off that blindfold and giving yourself a fighting chance at hitting the bullseye.

But not all goals are created equal. That's where SMART goals come in - a powerful framework that transforms vague wishes into concrete, achievable objectives. By using the SMART criteria, you'll craft goals that are clear, measurable, and aligned with your broader aspirations. This approach gives you a roadmap to success, ensuring that your goals are not just dreams, but actionable plans you can pursue with confidence.

Now, let's transform that vague wish into a concrete, actionable goal.

The Power of Writing It Down

Here's a little secret that successful people know there's immense power in putting pen to paper *(or fingers to keyboard)*. When you write down your goals, you're doing more than just recording them - you're making a commitment to yourself.

A study by Dr. Gail Matthews at Dominican University found that people who wrote down their goals were 42% more likely to achieve them than those who didn't. That's a massive difference from such a simple act!

But don't just write them down and forget about them. Make your goals visible. Put them on your bathroom mirror, set them as your phone background, or keep them in a journal you review daily. The more you see your goals, the more your subconscious mind works on making them a reality.

Daily Goal Review:

Speaking of reviewing your goals, let's talk about the power of daily goal review. This simple practice can be the difference between goals that gather dust and goals that gather momentum.

Every morning, before you dive into the chaos of the day, take 5 minutes to review your goals. Read them aloud, visualize yourself achieving them, and remind yourself why they matter to you. This daily ritual keeps your objectives front and center, guiding your decisions and actions throughout the day.

Ready to put this into practice?

Let's do it!

Exercise: Goal Setting Workshop

1. Identify a major goal you want to achieve in the next 6-12

months.

2. Use the SMART framework to refine your goal. Write it down in detail.
3. Break this goal down into smaller milestones (remember our 'Map Out Small Steps'?).
4. Write your goal and milestones on a piece of paper or in a digital note.
5. Set daily reminders to review your goal.
6. Each week, track your progress and adjust as needed.

Reflection Questions:

- How does having a SMART goal change your perspective on achieving it?
- What challenges do you anticipate in reaching this goal, and how can you prepare for them?
- How can you make your goal review a non-negotiable part of your daily routine?

Remember, setting clear objectives isn't just about achieving one goal - it's about training your mind to think in terms of specific, achievable outcomes. As you practice this skill, you'll find yourself naturally setting and achieving goals in all areas of your life.

In our next section, we'll explore how to add urgency and accountability to your goals with time-bound commitments.

T - TIME-BOUND Goals

We're about to dive deep into the world of time-bound commitments - the secret weapon that turns procrastinators into productivity powerhouses. Buckle up, because we're not just setting deadlines; we're unleashing a force that will catapult your goals from 'someday' dreams to 'right now' realities.

The Power of Deadlines

Have you ever wondered why you can accomplish so much in the days leading up to a vacation? That's the magic of deadlines at work. They create a sense of urgency that propels us into action, transforming vague "someday" goals into "right now" imperatives.

Psychologists have a name for this phenomenon: Parkinson's Law. It states that work expands to fill the time available for its completion. Without a deadline, tasks can stretch on indefinitely. But with a well-set deadline, we become focused, efficient, and driven.

Setting Realistic Deadlines

The key is to set deadlines that challenge you without overwhelming you. Here's how:

1. **Be Specific:** Instead of "I'll finish this project soon," try "I'll complete the first draft by 5 PM next Friday."
2. **Break It Down:** For long-term goals, set interim deadlines. If you're writing a book, you might aim to finish one chapter every two weeks.
3. **Consider Your Schedule:** Be realistic about your other commitments. Setting a deadline that conflicts with a busy period at work is setting yourself up for failure.
4. **Add a Buffer:** Things often take longer than we expect. Build in some extra time for unexpected challenges.

Time Management Tools

Leverage technology to keep your deadlines front and center:

1. **Digital Calendars:** Set deadline reminders that pop up on your phone or computer.
2. **Project Management Apps:** Tools like Trello or Asana can

help you visualize your deadlines and progress.

3. **Time-Tracking Apps:** Use apps like RescueTime to see how you're really spending your time and adjust accordingly.

Exercise: The Deadline Challenge

1. Choose a task you've been procrastinating on.
2. Set a realistic but challenging deadline for completing it.
3. Break the task down into smaller steps, each with its own mini deadline.

Reflection Questions:

- How did having a deadline affect your motivation and focus?
- What strategies helped you meet your deadline?
- How can you apply this to other areas of your life?

Remember, time-bound commitments aren't about adding stress to your life. They're about harnessing the natural power of urgency to propel you towards your goals. By setting thoughtful deadlines and holding yourself accountable to them, you're not just managing your time - you're taking control of your future.

In our next section, we'll explore how to face challenges head-on with the "I - Identify and Acknowledge" step of our MOTIVATE method.

Let's confront what's holding you back.

I - IDENTIFY and Acknowledge

In the journey of personal growth and goal achievement, we often encounter obstacles. Some are external, but many are internal - our fears, doubts, and limiting beliefs. This crucial step in the MOTIVATE framework is about shining a light on these challenges and confronting them head-on.

Why Identification Matters

Imagine trying to navigate a maze while blindfolded. That's what attempting to achieve your goals without identifying obstacles feels like. By clearly naming and acknowledging your challenges, you're taking off that blindfold. You're giving yourself the power to strategize and overcome.

The Power of Acknowledgment

Acknowledging challenges isn't about dwelling on negatives. It's about being honest with yourself. When you acknowledge a fear or a setback, you rob it of its power to operate in the shadows of your subconscious. You bring it into the light where you can examine it, understand it, and ultimately overcome it.

Steps to Identify and Acknowledge:

1. **Self-Reflection:** Take time to think deeply about what's holding you back. What fears come up when you think about your goals?
2. **Journaling:** Write down your thoughts and feelings. Often, the act of putting words on paper can bring clarity.
3. **Seek Feedback:** Sometimes, others can see our blind spots. Ask trusted friends or mentors what they think might be holding you back.
4. **Be Specific:** Instead of "I'm not good enough," try to pinpoint exactly what skill or knowledge you feel you're lacking.

5. **Avoid Self-Blame:** Remember, identifying challenges isn't about criticizing yourself. It's about gathering information to move forward.

Exercise: The Challenge Inventory

1. List your top three goals.
2. For each goal, write down at least three potential obstacles or challenges.
3. For each challenge, ask yourself: "What's the root cause of this obstacle?"
4. Acknowledge each challenge out loud, saying, "I acknowledge that [challenge] is holding me back from [goal]."

Reflection Questions:

- How did it feel to openly acknowledge your challenges?
- Were you surprised by any of the obstacles you identified?
- How can facing these challenges head-on help you in achieving your goals?

Remember that identifying and acknowledging challenges isn't about dwelling on negatives. It's about arming yourself with the information you need to create effective strategies. In our next section, we'll explore how to use this knowledge to validate your experiences and assess your path forward.

V - VALIDATE and Assess

Having identified your challenges, it's time to shift gears. The 'Validate and Assess' step is about extracting wisdom from your experiences and using it to fuel your growth. This isn't just about analyzing what went wrong – it's about recognizing the value in every step of your journey, even the missteps.

The Power of Validation

Validation isn't about seeking approval from others. It's about acknowledging your experiences, both positive and negative, as valid and valuable. When you validate your experiences, you're saying, "This happened, and it matters." This simple act can be incredibly empowering.

Assessing for Growth

Assessment isn't about judgment; it's about learning. Think of yourself as a scientist, objectively analyzing data from an experiment. Your experiences are that data, rich with insights if you know how to look for them.

Steps to Validate and Assess:

1. **Acknowledge Your Feelings:** Whatever you're feeling about your experiences is valid. Allow yourself to feel without judgment.
2. **Look for Patterns:** Are there recurring themes in your challenges? These patterns can offer valuable insights.
3. **Identify Lessons:** For each experience, ask yourself, "What can I learn from this?"
4. **Recognize Growth:** How have your challenges helped you develop new skills or strengths?
5. **Reframe Setbacks:** Instead of viewing setbacks as failures, see them as valuable feedback.

Exercise: The Experience Audit

1. Choose a recent challenge or setback related to your goals.
2. Write down the facts of what happened, as objectively as possible.
3. List the emotions you felt during and after this experience.
4. Identify at least three lessons or insights you can take from this experience.
5. Write a statement validating this experience: "This experience was valuable because..."

Reflection Questions:

- How does validating your experiences change your perspective on setbacks?
- What's the most surprising insight you've gained from assessing your experiences?
- How can you use these insights to adjust your approach moving forward?

Remember, every experience – whether it feels like a success or a failure in the moment – has the potential to propel you forward. In our next section, we'll explore how to take these insights and use them to adjust your approach. Are you ready to turn your experiences into your secret weapon for success? Let's dive into the 'Adjust and Adapt' step of our MOTIVATE journey!

A - ADJUST and Adapt

Life rarely follows our carefully laid plans. The ability to adjust and adapt isn't just a useful skill—it's essential for long-term success and wellbeing. This step in the MOTIVATE framework is about cultivating flexibility and resilience, allowing you to navigate life's inevitable twists and turns while staying true to your goals.

The Power of Flexibility

Rigidity breaks under pressure, but flexibility bends and bounces back. When you cultivate a flexible mindset, you're not easily derailed by unexpected challenges. Instead, you see them as opportunities to reassess, learn, and possibly discover even better paths to your goals.

Resilience: Your Success Superpower

Resilience is the ability to recover quickly from difficulties. It's not about avoiding stress or challenges, but about developing the capacity to deal with them effectively. With each challenge you overcome, your resilience grows, making you better equipped for future obstacles.

Strategies for Adjusting and Adapting:

1. **Embrace Change:** See change as an opportunity for growth rather than a threat.
2. **Stay Open-Minded:** Be willing to consider alternative approaches to reaching your goals.
3. **Practice Positive Self-Talk:** Replace "I can't do this" with "How can I approach this differently?"
4. **Learn from Others:** Seek advice from those who've successfully navigated similar challenges.
5. **Break It Down:** When faced with a big change, break it into smaller, manageable steps.

Exercise: The Adaptation Challenge

1. Identify a recent situation where things didn't go as planned.
2. List three ways you could have adjusted your approach in that situation.
3. Choose one of these alternative approaches and detail how you would implement it.
4. Reflect on how this new approach might lead to different (possibly better) outcomes.

Reflection Questions:

- How comfortable are you with change? How might increasing your comfort with change benefit you?
- Can you recall a time when an unexpected change led to a positive outcome?
- How can you build more flexibility into your goal-setting and planning processes?

Remember, adjusting and adapting isn't about giving up on your goals. It's about being smart and agile in your pursuit of them. By cultivating flexibility and resilience, you're not just preparing for challenges—you're setting yourself up to thrive in the face of them.

In our next section, we'll explore how to put all of this into action with the 'Take Action and Evaluate' step. Are you ready to turn your newfound adaptability into concrete results? Let's keep the momentum going in our MOTIVATE journey!

This section encourages readers to develop a flexible and resilient mindset, providing strategies and exercises to help them adapt to changes and challenges. It sets the stage for the next step in the MOTIVATE framework, where readers will learn how to take action based on their adjustments and evaluate their progress.

T - TAKE ACTION and Evaluate

Alright, goal-setter extraordinaire, it's time to turn those well-laid plans into real-world results. We've mapped our journey, set clear objectives, and prepared for challenges. Now comes the exciting part - taking action and seeing our efforts bear fruit!

The Power of Action

Ever heard the phrase "a journey of a thousand miles begins with a single step"? Well, it's not just a catchy saying - it's the secret sauce of achievement. Taking action, even in small doses, is like revving up the engine of success. Each step forward, no matter how tiny, builds momentum that can carry you through obstacles and over hurdles.

But here's the kicker - sometimes we get so caught up in planning and preparing that we never actually start. It's like spending hours packing for a trip but never leaving the house. This "analysis paralysis" can be a real motivation killer. So how do we break free? Simple: pick one small, achievable action and do it right now.

Consistent Execution

Now that we've kicked things off, let's talk about keeping the ball rolling. Consistent execution is the name of the game. Think of it like brushing your teeth - it's not always exciting, but do it regularly, and you'll see big benefits over time.

The key? Daily habits and routines. These are the building blocks of long-term success. Start small - maybe it's spending 15 minutes each morning working towards your goal. As this becomes second nature, you can gradually increase the time or complexity.

Here are some strategies to keep you on track:

1. **Use habit-stacking:** Attach your new habit to an existing one. For example, "After I pour my morning coffee, I'll spend 15

minutes on my project."

2. **Create a ritual:** Develop a specific sequence of actions that signal it's time to work on your goal. This could be as simple as lighting a candle or putting on your "focus" playlist.
3. **Track your streak:** Use a calendar or app to mark each day you complete your habit. You'll be motivated to keep your streak going!

Evaluation Techniques

Now, let's talk about keeping score. Regularly evaluating your progress is like having a GPS for your goals - it helps you see how far you've come and adjust your course as needed.

There are plenty of ways to track your progress:

1. **Journaling:** Take a few minutes each day or week to write about your actions and reflections.
2. **Apps:** Use goal-tracking apps to log your progress and visualize your journey.
3. **Regular check-ins:** Schedule weekly or monthly reviews to assess your advancement.

Remember, it's not just about the numbers. While quantitative measures (like how many pages you've written or pounds you've lost) are important, don't forget about qualitative evaluation. How do you feel about your progress? What have you learned? These insights are just as valuable as any metric.

Adjusting Course

Here's a truth bomb for you: no plan survives first contact with reality unchanged. And that's okay! In fact, it's expected. The key is to use your evaluations to inform your next steps.

Think of your journey like sailing a ship. You have a destination in mind, but winds and currents (life, in other words) might push you off course. Regular evaluations are like checking your map and compass. They help you see where you are and make necessary adjustments to get back on track.

Remember, achieving your goals isn't a straight line - it's an iterative process. Each cycle of action and evaluation brings you closer to your target, often in ways you might not have expected.

Exercise: The Action-Evaluation Cycle

1. Choose a goal you want to work on this week.
2. Plan one small action that you can take each day towards this goal.
3. At the end of each day, jot down what you did and how it went.
4. At the week's end, review your notes and reflect on these questions:
   ◦ What worked well?
   ◦ What challenges did you face?
   ◦ How do you feel about your progress?
   ◦ What will you do differently next week?

Reflection Questions:

- How did taking consistent action affect your motivation?
- What surprised you about the evaluation process?
- How can you use what you've learned to improve your approach next week?

Remember, every action, no matter how small, is a step forward. Every evaluation, no matter the outcome, is a chance to learn and grow. You've got this! Now, let's keep that momentum going as we dive into our final step: energizing ourselves with inspiration!

E - ENERGIZE with Inspiration

We've reached the final piece of our MOTIVATE puzzle. Now it's time to fuel your journey with an endless supply of inspiration and enthusiasm. Think of this as your secret weapon, your personal pep rally, your motivational mixtape. Let's dive in and light that inner fire!

Finding Your Why

You know those days when your alarm goes off and you think, "Why am I doing this again?" That's where your 'why' comes in. It's the heart and soul of your motivation, the deep-down reason that keeps you going when things get tough.

Your 'why' isn't just about achieving a goal; it's about connecting that goal to your core values and dreams. It's the difference between "I want to start a business" and "I want to create something that makes people's lives better and gives my family financial freedom."

Let's uncover your 'why' with a quick exercise:

- Write down your goal.
- Ask yourself, "Why is this important to me?" Write down the answer.
- Look at that answer and ask "Why?" again. Repeat this 3-5 times.

By the end, you should have drilled down to something that really resonates with your core values. That's your 'why', and it's more powerful than any to-do list or productivity hack.

Cultivating Inspiration

Now that we've tapped into your inner drive, let's talk about keeping that inspiration tank full. Think of inspiration as the premium fuel for your motivation engine. The more you have, the smoother and faster you'll run.

Here are some powerful ways to stay inspired:

1. **Success Stories:** Surround yourself with stories of triumph. Read biographies, watch documentaries, listen to podcasts about people who've achieved similar goals. Their journeys can light the way for yours.
2. **Vision Board:** Create a visual representation of your goals and dreams. Whether it's a physical board or a digital collage, fill it with images and words that represent your ideal future. Put it somewhere you'll see it every day.
3. **Motivational Content:** Find quotes, videos, or audio that fire you up. Create a playlist or a file of go-to content for when you need a boost.
4. **Positive People:** Surround yourself with enthusiastic, goal-oriented individuals. Their energy is contagious!

Remember, inspiration isn't just about feeling good; it's about creating a mindset where achieving your goals feels not just possible, but inevitable.

Celebrating Milestones

No victory is too small when you're on the path to greatness. Celebrating milestones isn't just fun (although it should be); it's a crucial part of maintaining long-term motivation. Each celebration reinforces your progress, boosts your confidence, and recharges your motivation batteries.

So, how do we celebrate? It doesn't have to be a grand party (unless that's your style).

It could be:

- Treating yourself to something special
- Sharing your achievement with supportive friends or family
- Taking a day off to relax and reflect on your progress
- Adding a gold star to your calendar or tracker

The key is to acknowledge your progress in a way that feels meaningful to you. Remember, you're not just celebrating what you've achieved; you're celebrating who you're becoming.

Overcoming Motivation Dips

Let's get real for a moment, because even with all these strategies, there will be days when your motivation takes a nosedive. It's not a matter of if, but when. The good news? These dips are totally normal and completely conquerable.

Common motivation killers include:

- Burnout from overworking
- Setbacks or perceived failures
- Losing sight of your 'why'
- Comparison with others

When you feel your motivation flagging, try these revival techniques:

1. **Revisit your 'why':** Reconnect with your core reasons for pursuing this goal.
2. **Break it down:** Sometimes we get overwhelmed by the big picture. Focus on just the next small step.

Change your environment: A new workspace or even a quick walk can shift your perspective.

Seek support: Reach out to a friend, mentor, or support group for encouragement.

Practice self-compassion: Be kind to yourself. Motivation dips are part of the journey, not a reflection of your worth or potential.

Exercise: The Inspiration Board

Let's create your personal motivation machine:

1. Choose your medium: physical board, mind map, or even a dedicated notebook.
2. Collect inspiring images, quotes, and personal mantras that align with your goals and values.
3. Add representations of your achievements so far, no matter how small.
4. Include photos or symbols of people who inspire you.
5. Place your board where you'll see it daily.
6. Spend a few minutes each morning connecting with your board, letting it energize you for the day ahead.

Reflection Questions:

- What's one thing on your inspiration board that really fires you up? Why?

- How can you make celebration a regular part of your goal-achieving process?
- What's your go-to strategy for rekindling your motivation when it dips?

Remember, motivation isn't something you find; it's something you create and nurture every day. With these tools in your MOTIVATE toolkit, you're not just prepared for the journey ahead – you're ready to absolutely rock it.

Now, armed with your supercharged mindset and overflowing inspiration, you're all set to take on whatever challenges come your way. The path to your dreams is clear, and you've got everything you need to walk it.

The Peaks of Purposeful Progress

———

As you finish reading the MOTIVATE YOUR MINDSET chapter, the principles echo in your mind. A newfound clarity begins to take shape. It hits you – these aren't just random ideas, but a roadmap to reclaiming your headspace. A roadmap you are ready to follow:

Your journey of motivation begins to unfold.

1. You begin by Mapping Out small steps, breaking down your goals into manageable tasks. This transforms overwhelming goals into achievable milestones, instantly shifting your state from anxious to empowered.
2. With your path clearer, you move on to Objective Setting. Here, you craft clear, compelling goals that resonate with your deepest values, further energizing your emotional state.
3. To maintain momentum, you create Time-Bound Commitments. By adding deadlines to your objectives, you infuse your plan with a sense of urgency, keeping your motivational state high.
4. As you progress, you start Investigating patterns in your behavior and emotional responses. This self-awareness allows you to identify what triggers both positive and negative states.
5. Next, you practice Validating and assessing your progress. This step reinforces positive states by acknowledging your achievements, no matter how small.
6. Life is unpredictable, so you learn the art of Adjusting and adapting. This flexibility helps you maintain a positive state even when faced with unexpected challenges.
7. Armed with knowledge and a plan, you focus on Taking

action. This step is crucial in creating and maintaining motivated states through the power of momentum.

8. Finally, you discover techniques for Energizing yourself with inspiration. This ensures you can access empowering states at will, fueling your journey towards your goals.

You realize that these steps form a continuous cycle, each feeding into the next, creating a self-reinforcing system for maintaining high motivation and positive mental states. With this framework, you feel equipped to tackle any challenge, knowing you have the tools to manage your state and keep moving forward.

Reality shifts once more, revealing a grand challenge.

Suddenly, the world around you begins to shift.

The room fades away, and you find yourself at the base of a majestic mountain range—the Peaks of Purposeful Progress. Each mountain represents a different aspect of the MOTIVATE framework, challenging you to apply what you've learned.

As you survey the landscape, a wise guide appears beside you. "Welcome," they say, "to the journey of motivation. Each peak you conquer will strengthen your mindset and bring you closer to your goals. Are you ready to begin?"

Your ascent begins with small, manageable steps.

You nod, determination filling your heart. The first mountain looms before you, its winding path representing the 'Map out small steps' principle.

As you begin your ascent, you notice the path is marked with small, achievable goals. Each step forward feels manageable, and you find yourself making steady progress. You realize that breaking down your larger goal of reaching the summit into these smaller steps makes the journey less daunting.

An ancient artifact offers a new perspective.

Reaching the first peak, you pause to catch your breath, marveling at the view before you. The next mountain looms ahead, its summit marked by a glinting beacon that catches your eye. This peak, you realize, represents 'Objective setting' from the MOTIVATE framework.

As you prepare for the next leg of your journey, you notice something unusual beside the path - a weathered brass telescope mounted on a sturdy tripod. Its antique appearance suggests it has witnessed countless climbers' journeys. Attached to it is a small, age-worn tag with a cryptic message:

"To see your goal, you must first look beyond the obvious. Adjust your vision, and your path will become clear."

The telescope reveals hidden truths about your journey.

Intrigued, you approach the telescope. As you peer through its lens, you're surprised to find that it doesn't merely magnify the distant summit. Instead, it seems to reveal hidden aspects of the path ahead - obstacles, shortcuts, and resting points that were invisible to the naked eye.

This, you realize, is a powerful metaphor for the objective-setting process. Just as the telescope helps you see the journey more clearly, setting clear objectives allows you to visualize your path to success, anticipating challenges and identifying opportunities along the way.

Your goals come into sharp focus.

As you adjust the focus, you begin to see your own goals reflected in the landscape before you. The beacon at the summit transforms, taking on the shape of your personal objectives. This vivid visualization fills you with a sense of purpose and determination.

A newfound clarity propels you forward.

You step back from the telescope, your mind buzzing with newfound clarity. The next phase of your climb now feels less daunting and more purposeful. You understand that, like adjusting the telescope's focus, setting clear objectives requires careful consideration and occasional readjustment.

With this new perspective, you begin your descent towards the next challenge, eager to see how the remaining elements of the MOTIVATE framework will manifest in your journey.

Reflection: What is one clear, specific objective you can set for yourself in the coming week?

Time becomes tangible as you face the third peak.

The third peak looms before you, representing 'Time-bound commitments.' As you approach, you notice a series of hourglasses embedded in the rock face, each filled with shimmering sand. A weathered plaque nearby reads:

"Choose your time wisely. Each grain of sand is a moment you'll never get back."

The weight of time spurs you to action.

You select an hourglass, feeling its weight as you clip it to your belt. Immediately, a sense of urgency courses through you. The steadily falling sand creates a palpable deadline, spurring you to climb with renewed focus and efficiency.

This time-bound challenge pushes you to make swift decisions and maximize every movement. As you ascend, you realize how this pressure, while intense, is also oddly motivating. It's a visceral reminder of how deadlines can drive action and achievement.

Reflection: How can you create meaningful deadlines for your goals to maintain momentum?

Your journey replays, revealing hidden patterns.

Captivated, you watch as the mountain's surface displays a mesmerizing replay of your climb. You see yourself repeatedly favoring certain footholds, doubting the choices you made at each fork, and alternating between bursts of energy and moments of fatigue. These recurring patterns, previously unnoticed, now stand out in stark relief.

Self-awareness becomes your new superpower.

This visual retrospective offers a unique vantage point, allowing you to step back and analyze your journey objectively. As you study these patterns, you begin to recognize how your instinctive choices and habitual behaviors have shaped your ascent, for better or worse. This newfound self-awareness feels like a powerful tool, one that you can leverage to optimize your approach for the challenges that lie ahead.

How will these insights shape your future climbs?

As you approach the next peak, 'Validate and assess,' you encounter a series of ancient stone arches. Each arch bears a weathered plaque with a puzzling inscription.

Riddles prompt deep introspection.

The first arch's riddle reads: *"What decision on your climb, if changed, would have altered your path the most?"* As you ponder this, you're compelled to revisit your choices, assessing their impact on your journey.

Passing through, you reach the second arch. Its puzzle asks: *"Name three obstacles you've overcome and the strengths they revealed in you."* This prompts you to acknowledge your progress and the personal growth you've achieved.

Each puzzle deepens your self-understanding.

With each arch, you find yourself diving deeper into self-reflection, validating your achievements and critically assessing your approach. These moments of contemplation provide a natural rhythm to gauge your progress objectively.

Accomplishment fuels your resolve.

As you solve each puzzle, a sense of accomplishment washes over you, reinforcing your resolve for the challenges ahead. You realize that this process of continuous evaluation and acknowledgment is a powerful tool, not just for this climb, but for all of life's journeys.

This experience underscores the value of regular self-assessment, demonstrating how it can bolster motivation and guide continuous improvement in any endeavor.

Reflection: How often do you stop to assess your progress? How might more frequent evaluation improve your results?

As you begin your ascent of the 'Adjust and adapt' peak, the mountain seems to come alive with challenges. The once-clear path splinters into a maze of unexpected twists and turns. Suddenly, the sky darkens and a fierce wind whips around you. Rockslides cascade down the slopes, forcing you to quickly alter your route. Hidden crevasses appear without warning, testing your reflexes and resolve.

External and internal obstacles test your adaptability.

You realize this peak embodies life's unpredictability, demanding not just physical agility, but mental and emotional flexibility as well. As you navigate these external obstacles, internal struggles surface. Self-doubt whispers in your ear, the incline feels impossibly steep, and your energy begins to flag.

The MOTIVATE framework becomes your compass.

In this moment of crisis, you recall the MOTIVATE framework. You remember that true adaptability isn't just about external circumstances—it's also about managing your internal state. Taking a deep breath, you mentally revisit each component of MOTIVATE:

- You Map out small steps to navigate the immediate challenges
- You remind yourself of your Objective: reaching the summit
- You set a Time-bound commitment to reassess your situation in 10 minutes
- You Identify and acknowledge your current struggles
- You Validate your progress so far, despite the setbacks
- You're actively Adjusting and adapting to the mountain's challenges
- You Take action, making decisive moves despite the uncertainty
- You Energize yourself by visualizing the view from the summit

Renewed determination propels you forward.

This mental exercise re-centers your thoughts and renews your determination. With a clearer mind and a flexible approach, you continue your ascent, ready to adapt to whatever the mountain—and life—may throw your way.

What other challenges await you on this journey, and how will you adapt to overcome them?

How can you harness the power of the MOTIVATE framework to navigate not only the physical obstacles but also the internal struggles that may arise?

Reflection: Can you recall a time when adapting your approach led to unexpected positive outcomes?

The power of decisive action reveals itself.

The near-final peak looms before you, embodying 'Take Action.' As you approach, the path splinters into multiple routes, each promising a different journey to the summit. A weathered signpost stands at the fork, bearing a simple message: "Choose, then climb."

You pause, weighing your options. The MOTIVATE framework echoes in your mind, reminding you that while planning is crucial, it's action that propels you forward. Taking a deep breath, you select a path and begin your ascent with purposeful strides.

Each step becomes a testament to progress.

As you climb, you realize that each step, no matter how small, is progress. The act of moving forward, of taking action, energizes you in a way that mere planning never could. This peak teaches you the power of decisiveness and the importance of momentum in achieving your goals.

Finally, you reach the last and highest peak, 'Energize with inspiration.' The summit greets you with a breathtaking panorama of your entire journey. Each peak you've conquered stands as a testament to your growth and resilience.

The mountain air invigorates your spirit.

The crisp mountain air fills your lungs, invigorating you with each breath. The wind whips at your face, a tangible reminder of the challenges you've overcome and the progress you've made. Your heart pounds with exhilaration, its rhythm matching the triumphant tempo of your climb.

The Summit's Hidden Wisdom

As you reach the summit, your eyes catch a glimpse of a small, weathered box nestled in a sheltered nook of the rocky terrain. It blends seamlessly with the mountain, almost as if it belongs there. Intrigued, you carefully lift the lid.

Inside, you discover a leather-bound journal and a solid, well-made pen, both surprisingly well-preserved despite the harsh conditions. A weathered note lies atop the journal, reading:

"Fellow climber, share your journey here. The reflections of today will guide tomorrow's climb."

Reflection transforms experience into wisdom.

As you write, recounting each peak and the lessons learned, you feel a profound sense of motivation and purpose washing over you. You realize that this journey through the MOTIVATE peaks has not just been about reaching a destination, but about becoming someone new—someone more capable, more resilient, and more inspired.

Your transformation is complete.

You close the journal, knowing that the insights and energy you've gained will fuel your future endeavors. The MOTIVATE framework is no longer just a concept, but a lived experience etched into your very being. As you prepare for your descent, you're filled with anticipation for how you'll apply these lessons in the world below.

Reflection: What inspires and energizes you? How can you incorporate more of these elements into your daily life?

As the majestic peaks fade from view, you find yourself back in familiar surroundings, profoundly transformed. The MOTIVATE framework is no longer an abstract concept but a lived experience, etched into the very fabric of your being.

A new challenge emerges on the horizon.

A surge of purpose electrifies your spirit, illuminating the path ahead with newfound clarity. Challenges that once seemed insurmountable now appear as opportunities to apply your hard-won wisdom. As you close the book, a new question emerges, bridging your mountain adventure with the realities of daily life:

"How will this newfound motivation and clarity guide me through the challenges of the midday hours, when energy often wanes and distractions multiply?"

Your journey continues, with new tools at your disposal.

The journey to mastering your 24 hours continues, and you sense that the next chapter holds the key to maintaining your momentum when the day threatens to drag you down. Your adventure through the Peaks of Purposeful Progress hasn't just equipped you with tools; it has forged you into a master of motivation, ready to face the inevitable ebbs and flows of each day.

Anticipation builds for the next challenge.

As you turn the page, anticipation builds. The midday hours, once a dreaded battleground against fatigue and distraction, now beckon as an exciting proving ground for your newfound resilience. You're eager to discover how to harness this MOTIVATE-powered momentum, to alchemize potential slumps into surges of productivity, and to create a rhythm that sustains you from dawn till dusk.

You stand ready to thrive through every hour.

The next phase of your journey awaits, promising to reveal the secrets of maintaining your drive when others falter. You're ready to embrace this challenge, armed with the unwavering belief that you can thrive—not just survive—through every hour of your day.

With a deep breath and a determined smile, you begin the next chapter, "YOUR MIDDAY MOMENTUM," prepared to transform the toughest part of your day into your most productive hours.

YOUR MIDDAY MOMENTUM

"Transform your day into a masterpiece of productivity and fulfillment."

After unlocking the power of a motivated mindset in our last chapter, where we harnessed the mental energy needed to kickstart our day, it's time to channel that momentum into the afternoon. Welcome to YOUR MIDDAY MOMENTUM. This chapter is dedicated to sustaining and amplifying the morning's spark, transforming the afternoon into a period of peak productivity and fulfillment. The groundwork has been laid; now we'll elevate your daily routine with the THRIVE Framework, ensuring that every moment from morning to night is infused with purpose and efficiency.

As you reflect on the MOTIVATE framework and your journey through the Peaks of Purposeful Progress, you might wonder:

How will your newfound motivation techniques adapt to the unique challenges of midday?

We've all encountered it—that post-lunch slump where the morning's energy wanes, and it feels like you're hitting a wall. This is a pivotal moment. How you navigate these next few hours can determine whether you end the day feeling accomplished or drained. But what if we could turn that midday challenge into a powerful advantage?

"Your Midday Momentum" isn't about fighting against fatigue or ignoring the natural rhythms of your body and mind. It's about embracing these rhythms, optimizing your energy, and aligning your actions with your deepest values and most ambitious goals.

The THRIVE Framework is a transformative approach that goes beyond simple time management tips. THRIVE is a comprehensive system designed to elevate your afternoons and supercharge your entire day. It's not just about getting through the afternoon; it's about creating a second wind that propels you to a strong and satisfying finish.

Later in the Summit of Sustained Success, your mastery of the THRIVE Framework will be put to the test in ways you can't yet imagine. You'll face real-world challenges that demand you apply everything you've learned. Are you ready to climb to new heights of productivity?

Let's dive into how you can harness this framework to keep your momentum soaring.

The THRIVE Framework:

To help you master your midday momentum and elevate your entire day, let's introduce the THRIVE Framework:

1. **T**ransform your routines
2. **H**armonize your actions with your goals

3. Revitalize your energy
4. Investigate your patterns
5. Visualize your success
6. Execute with focus and flexibility

While each element of THRIVE is powerful on its own, their true strength lies in how they interlock and build upon each other. As you master one aspect, you'll find the others becoming more natural and effective.

How will this synergy manifest in your daily life?

Imagine ending each day feeling accomplished, energized, and eager for tomorrow's opportunities. Picture yourself navigating challenges with grace, turning potential slumps into periods of incredible productivity. This is the power of mastering your midday momentum.

While the MOTIVATE framework was about setting the stage with a positive mindset, THRIVE is about actionable steps to keep that momentum going. This isn't just about avoiding the afternoon slump; it's about transforming the middle part of your day into a powerhouse of productivity and joy.

Let's explore each component of the THRIVE Framework in depth.

T – TRANSFORM Your Routines for Peak Performance

Transforming your midday isn't just about tweaking your schedule; it's about revolutionizing how you approach the heart of your day. This transformation is a strategic shift, not just a minor adjustment.

Imagine hitting your stride just as others are slowing down, turning what's often the most challenging part of the day into your most productive hours. Whether it's through reassessment, strategic planning, or habit reformation, transforming your midday routines sets the stage for sustained success.

Think of this transformation as a pivot point in your day, where you consciously redirect your energy and focus. This is the moment where you reassess, realign, and recommit to your goals. It's about creating a second wind that carries you through to a strong finish.

Recharge and Refocus:

- Pause to reassess your progress, like a climber taking a breather
- Review your to-do list and goals for the day
- Evaluate your energy levels honestly
- Note any unexpected obstacles that have arisen

Strategic Adjustment:

- Reprioritize tasks based on your reassessment
- Adjust your pace to match your energy levels
- Alter your approach to accommodate new challenges
- Ensure you're moving purposefully towards your daily goals

Habit Reformation:

- Identify patterns that may hinder your progress, like midday slumps
- Experiment with different timings and activities for better productivity
- Create new habits that rejuvenate and energize you
- Observe how small changes can have unexpected positive effects on your day

How might a small change in your midday routine impact your evening productivity or even your sleep quality?

Exercise: For the next week, commit to a 5-minute midday reset. At lunchtime, review your morning's accomplishments, adjust your afternoon plan, and set one key intention for the rest of the day. After the week, reflect on how this routine has impacted your productivity and overall satisfaction.

Reflection: How do the MOTIVATE techniques you learned earlier support your midday transformation? Can you see a connection between your morning motivation and afternoon momentum?

Remember, the goal of transformation is not perfection but progress. Even small shifts in how you approach your midday can lead to significant improvements in your daily productivity and satisfaction. As you continue to refine your transformation routine, you'll discover what works best for you, creating a personalized approach to making every afternoon count.

As we transition from transforming your routines, let's explore how to harmonize your actions with your goals and values. This alignment is crucial for maintaining momentum and finding fulfillment in your daily pursuits.

H – HARMONIZE Your Actions and Goals

Harmonizing is about creating a seamless connection between what you do and what truly matters to you. It's the process of ensuring that your midday activities are in tune with your broader objectives and personal values.

Here's how to achieve this harmony:

1. **Revisit Your Priorities:** Take a moment to reconnect with

your core goals and values. Ask yourself:

- What are my top three priorities for today?
- How do these align with my long-term objectives?
- Am I spending time on what truly matters?

This brief reflection helps recenter your focus on what's genuinely important.

1. **Align Your Tasks:** Look at your remaining to-do list for the day. For each task, consider:

- How does this contribute to my main goals?
- Is this the best use of my time right now?
- Can I delegate or postpone any tasks that don't align with my priorities?

Be willing to adjust your plans if you find misalignment.

1. **Create Meaningful Moments:** Find ways to infuse more purpose into your afternoon:

- Can you turn a routine task into a learning experience?
- Is there a chance to collaborate with others on a shared goal?
- How can you add value to others through your work?

These small shifts can transform mundane activities into meaningful contributions.

Exercise: For the next three days, spend two minutes at midday writing down your top three priorities for the rest of the day. Ensure each priority directly supports one of your broader life or career goals. At the end of each day, reflect on how well your actions aligned with these priorities.

Reflection:

1. How does aligning your daily actions with your broader goals affect your motivation and satisfaction?
2. What are the most common sources of misalignment in your day, and how can you address them?
3. In what ways can you create more harmony between your personal values and your professional responsibilities?

By harmonizing your actions with your goals, you create a sense of purpose and direction that can carry you through the challenges of the afternoon. This alignment not only boosts productivity but also enhances your overall sense of fulfillment and progress.

Imagine aligning your actions with your goals while navigating treacherous terrain. How might the stakes of a challenging climb amplify the importance of harmonization?

As we move from harmonizing your actions with your goals, it's crucial to address the physical and mental energy needed to execute these aligned tasks effectively. This brings us to the next vital part of the THRIVE framework: Revitalize.

R – REVITALIZE Your Energy Levels

Midday often brings a natural dip in energy, but with the right strategies, you can counteract this slump and maintain your momentum. Revitalizing isn't about pushing through fatigue; it's about strategically refreshing your mind and body to sustain your focus and productivity.

Here are some ways to revitalize your energy:

1. **Nutritional Boost:** What you eat significantly impacts your afternoon energy levels.

- Opt for a balanced lunch with lean proteins, complex carbohydrates, and healthy fats.
- Stay hydrated. Even mild dehydration can lead to fatigue.
- Consider a small, nutrient-rich snack if you feel your energy waning.

1. **Physical Recharge:** Brief physical activity can dramatically boost your energy and mental clarity.

- Take a short walk, ideally outdoors if possible.
- Do a few minutes of stretching or simple desk exercises.
- If possible, consider a power nap of 10-20 minutes.

1. **Mental Refresh:** Give your brain a chance to reset and refocus.

- Practice a brief meditation or mindfulness exercise.
- Engage in a quick brainstorming session on a project you're passionate about.
- Switch tasks to something that requires a different type of mental engagement.

Exercise: For the next week, implement a 10-minute revitalization break in the early afternoon. Rotate through different activities: one day focus on nutrition, the next on physical activity, and the third on mental refreshment. Note which strategies have the most significant impact on your afternoon energy and productivity.

Reflection:

1. How do different revitalization techniques affect your energy levels and focus?
2. What are your personal signs of an impending energy slump,

and how can you proactively address them?

3. In what ways can you tailor your revitalization strategies to fit your specific work environment and schedule?

By actively revitalizing your energy levels, you set yourself up for a productive and focused afternoon. This isn't about constant high-intensity output, but rather about maintaining a steady, sustainable level of engagement throughout your day.

As we transition from revitalizing your energy, it's important to understand how these efforts fit into your overall productivity patterns. This brings us to the next part of the THRIVE framework: Investigate.

I – INVESTIGATE Productivity Patterns

Investigating your productivity patterns isn't about self-criticism; it's about gaining valuable insights into how you work best. By understanding your unique rhythms and tendencies, you can make informed decisions about how to structure your afternoons for optimal performance.

Here's how to effectively investigate your productivity patterns:

1. **Track Your Output:** Start by monitoring your productivity throughout the day.

- Record when you complete tasks and how long they take.
- Pay attention to the quality of your work at different times.
- Identify periods of high focus and moments when your attention wanders.

1. **Analyze Your Environment:** Consider how your surroundings affect your work.

- Observe how different noise levels impact your concentration.
- Note the effects of lighting, temperature, and workspace organization on your productivity.
- Recognize how interactions with colleagues influence your focus and energy.

1. **Reflect on Internal Factors:** Examine how your personal state affects your performance.

- Monitor how your mood fluctuates throughout the day.
- Consider how different types of tasks affect your motivation.
- Reflect on how your sleep, diet, and exercise habits influence your afternoon performance.

Exercise: For one week, keep a simple productivity journal. At the end of each hour, quickly jot down what you accomplished, your energy level (high, medium, low), and any factors that significantly impacted your work. At the end of the week, review your notes to identify patterns.

Reflection:

1. What surprising insights have you gained about your productivity patterns?
2. How can you leverage your peak performance times to tackle your most important tasks?
3. What small changes in your environment or habits could potentially lead to significant improvements in your afternoon productivity?

By investigating your performance insights, you equip yourself with the knowledge to make strategic decisions about your work habits. This self-awareness is a powerful tool for continuous improvement, allowing you to refine your approach and maximize your productive potential.

Having gained insights into your productivity patterns, the next step is to use this information to shape your vision for success. This brings us to the fifth part of the THRIVE framework: Visualize.

V – VISUALIZE Your Peak Performance

Visualization is a powerful tool used by athletes, executives, and high achievers across various fields. It's not about daydreaming; it's about mentally rehearsing your ideal performance to prime yourself for success.

Here's how to effectively visualize your peak performance:

1. **Create a Clear Mental Image:** Picture yourself navigating your afternoon at your absolute best.

   - Imagine tackling your tasks with focus and efficiency.
   - See yourself handling challenges with calm and creativity.
   - Envision the satisfaction of ending your day having accomplished your key goals.

1. **Engage Multiple Senses:** Remember to make your visualization as vivid as possible.

   - What does your productive workspace look and feel like?
   - How does it feel to be in a state of flow as you work?
   - What sounds are present in your ideal work environment?

1. **Rehearse Specific Scenarios:** Use visualization to prepare for

upcoming tasks or challenges.

- Mentally walk through the steps of an important project.
- Imagine successfully navigating potential obstacles.
- Visualize positive interactions with colleagues or clients.

Exercise: Before starting your afternoon work, take 5 minutes to visualize your ideal productive afternoon. Be as specific as possible, imagining yourself moving through your tasks with ease and purpose. At the end of the day, compare your actual performance to your visualization. Note any differences and consider how you might adjust your approach.

Reflection:

1. How does visualization impact your motivation and confidence in tackling afternoon tasks?
2. In what ways can you make your visualizations more detailed and effective?
3. How might regular visualization practice influence your long-term productivity and goal achievement?

By visualizing your peak performance, you set a clear intention for your afternoon and prime your mind for success. This practice can help bridge the gap between your current habits and your ideal productivity, guiding you towards consistent high performance.

With a clear vision of your peak performance in mind, it's time to put everything into action. This brings us to the final component of the THRIVE framework: Execute.

E – EXECUTE with Adaptive Focus

Execution is where all the previous elements come together. It's about taking decisive action while remaining flexible enough to adapt to changing circumstances. This balance of focus and adaptability is key to maintaining momentum throughout your afternoon.

Here's how to execute effectively:

1. **Prioritize and Start:** Begin with your most important task.

- Use the insights from your investigation and visualization to tackle your priority items.
- Apply the "two-minute rule": If a task takes less than two minutes, do it immediately.
- Break larger tasks into smaller, manageable steps to avoid feeling overwhelmed.

1. **Maintain Focus:** Use techniques to stay on track.

- Implement the Pomodoro Technique: Work in focused 25-minute intervals followed by short breaks.
- Minimize distractions: Close unnecessary tabs, silence notifications, and create a focused environment.
- Use your revitalization strategies to maintain energy and concentration.

1. **Adapt as Needed:** Be prepared to adjust your plan.

- Regularly check in with your priorities and progress.
- Be willing to shift focus if urgent matters arise but do so consciously and strategically.
- Use unexpected free time productively by having a list of important but non-urgent tasks ready.

Exercise: For the next three afternoons, choose one significant task to complete. Break it down into 25-minute Pomodoro sessions. After each session, briefly note what you accomplished and any adjustments you made to your approach. At the end of the three days, review your notes to see how your execution improved.

Reflection:

1. How does breaking tasks into focused intervals affect your productivity and sense of accomplishment?
2. What are your most common distractions, and how can you more effectively manage them?
3. In what ways has your ability to adapt while maintaining focus improved since implementing the THRIVE framework?

Effective execution is the culmination of all your efforts in the THRIVE framework. By applying adaptive focus, you're not just working harder; you're working smarter. This approach allows you to maintain your midday momentum, turning your afternoons into a powerful driver of your daily success.

As you reflect on these strategies, a new challenge looms on the horizon. How will these techniques fare when pushed to their limits? Are you ready to test your newfound skills in a high-stakes environment where every decision counts?

The Summit of Sustained Success awaits, promising to put your mastery of the THRIVE framework to the ultimate test. As you turn the page, prepare yourself for an adventure that will challenge you to apply these principles in ways you never imagined. Will you rise to the occasion and conquer the peak of productivity, or will the pressures of this monumental task overwhelm you?

Summit of Sustained Success

———

In the quiet of the early afternoon, with "The Power of 24 Hours" open before you, you ponder the intricacies of the THRIVE Framework. As you contemplate how to maintain your midday momentum, your surroundings begin to shift. The familiar confines of your office fade into a swirling mist.

A challenging hiking trail appears before you.

As your vision clears, you find yourself at the start of a steep hiking trail—the Summit of Sustained Success. This path, with its ups and downs, reflects the natural fluctuations in your daily productivity. The varied landscape ahead represents the different aspects of the THRIVE Framework you've just learned, and now it's time to put them to the test.

As you begin your ascent, you're immediately confronted with a challenging incline. The steep path ahead mirrors the intense demands of your typical midday, when energy often wanes and focus wavers. It's here that the 'Transform' element of THRIVE becomes crucial.

Pausing to catch your breath, you reassess your approach. The daunting climb before you seems overwhelming, but you recall the lessons of THRIVE. Just as you've learned to transform your daily routines, you now break down this ascent into manageable segments. This strategic adjustment embodies the essence of adaptation for optimal performance.

As you progress, you encounter a series of unexpected detours. These winding paths seem to lead you away from the summit, testing your resolve. Each turn requires you to reassess and adjust your strategy, much like navigating the unpredictable twists in your daily life. You realize that this constant need for adaptation is precisely what the 'Transform' element prepares you for – the ability to adjust your course without losing sight of your ultimate goal.

Reflection: How has transforming your midday routines impacted your overall productivity? What new strategies will you apply to navigate this challenging ascent?

As you navigate a particularly challenging stretch of terrain, you're suddenly halted by an unexpected obstacle – a fresh rockslide has completely blocked your planned route. This moment perfectly encapsulates the 'Harmonize' component of THRIVE, challenging you to realign your actions with your ultimate goal.

A detour reveals unexpected beauty.

Taking a deep breath, you survey your surroundings, searching for an alternative path. The detour you spot seems daunting at first – a narrow, less-traveled trail that winds precariously along the mountain's edge. As you cautiously make your way along this new route, you're rewarded with breathtaking vistas that were hidden from your original path. This unexpected beauty reminds you of how adapting to life's obstacles can often lead to unforeseen rewards.

A cry for help tests your values.

Your moment of appreciation is interrupted by calls for help. A small group of fellow climbers appears to be struggling, one of them nursing what looks like a sprained ankle. This unexpected situation presents a dilemma that tests the true essence of 'Harmonize' – how do you balance your drive to reach the summit with your innate compassion to help others in need?

Your choices reflect your deepest values.

This challenge mirrors the daily choices we face, where our actions must align with our values. Helping these climbers will undoubtedly slow your ascent and potentially jeopardize your goal of reaching the summit before the incoming storm. Yet, the compassionate part of you recognizes that true success isn't just about personal achievement; it's about extending kindness and support to those who need it.

As you weigh your options, you realize that this is precisely what 'Harmonize' prepares you for – finding balance between competing priorities and ensuring your actions reflect your broader life values, not just your immediate goals.

Reflection: How has your ability to harmonize your actions with your goals improved your midday performance? Can you recall a recent situation where successfully aligning your efforts led to unforeseen positive outcomes?

After your compassionate detour, you reach a plateau that presents a new challenge – a crossroads where fatigue sets in, mirroring that all-too-familiar afternoon slump where your energy and focus start to dwindle. This junction embodies the 'Revitalize' aspect of THRIVE, calling on you to rejuvenate your depleted resources.

You reach a critical juncture in your climb.

Recognizing the critical nature of this moment, you consciously apply your revitalization techniques. You hydrate thoroughly, perform a series of quick yet effective stretches, and fuel up with a nutrient-rich snack from your pack. As you feel energy coursing back through your body, you're reminded of how these small but purposeful actions can dramatically shift your state, both on the mountain and in your daily life.

Your awareness sharpens as you investigate your patterns.

Invigorated, you press on, now acutely aware of how the changing terrain impacts your pace and energy levels. This heightened consciousness represents the 'Investigate' element of THRIVE. You begin to analyze your patterns meticulously – noting how the rocky inclines challenge your endurance but spark your problem-solving skills, while the monotonous flat stretches test your mental fortitude.

Doubt creeps in as the summit nears.

As you near the summit, the air thins noticeably, and doubt starts to creep in. The peak, now visible but still daunting, demands that you employ the 'Visualize' element of THRIVE. Pausing briefly, you close your eyes and vividly picture yourself conquering the final ascent. You imagine the exhilaration of reaching the top, the sense of accomplishment flooding through you. This powerful mental image acts as a catalyst, renewing your determination and dispelling the creeping doubts.

The final push integrates all you've learned.

With a deep breath and sharpened focus, you launch into the final push. This last leg of your journey represents the 'Execute' part of THRIVE. Here, you seamlessly integrate all the strategies you've honed – transforming your approach as the terrain demands, harmonizing your actions with your ultimate goal, tapping into your revitalized energy reserves, leveraging the insights from your self-investigation, and drawing strength from your vivid visualization.

Success reveals a new perspective on productivity.

At last, you crest the final ridge. The summit is yours. As you stand atop the peak, a breathtaking panorama unfolds before you. This awe-inspiring vista is more than just a view – it represents the comprehensive perspective you've gained through mastering the

THRIVE Protocol. From this vantage point, you can see both the soaring peaks of productivity and the necessary valleys of rest and rejuvenation that comprise a well-lived life.

Reflection: Looking back on your journey, how has the THRIVE framework most significantly improved your midday momentum? How will you apply these insights to maintain peak performance throughout your entire day?

Your descent becomes a reflection on lessons learned.

As you begin your descent, you carry with you more than just the triumph of reaching the summit. You've gained a profound understanding of how to navigate the complex terrain of sustained productivity in your everyday life. The THRIVE Protocol has transformed from an abstract concept into a lived experience, now woven into the very fabric of your daily approach.

Each step reinforces a key component of THRIVE.

Each step down the mountain reminds you of a lesson learned:

- A tricky detour recalls the importance of Transforming your routines.
- A moment of helping a fellow climber echoes the need to Harmonize your actions with your values.
- A rest stop mirrors the crucial practice of Revitalizing your energy.
- The varied terrain reinforces the value of Investigating your patterns.
- A challenging stretch brings to mind the power of Visualizing success.
- And the final push to the summit embodies the necessity of Executing with focus and flexibility.

You return, changed and ready for new challenges.

As you return to the familiar rhythms of your life, you find yourself fundamentally changed. The midday slumps that once seemed insurmountable now appear as opportunities for revitalization and renewed focus. You're ready to tackle whatever comes next, armed with the comprehensive strategy of THRIVE and the confidence born from conquering the Summit of Sustained Success.

You feel transformed by your journey through the Summit of Sustained Success. The THRIVE framework is no longer just a concept, but a lived experience woven into the fabric of your approach to each day. You're ready to tackle whatever comes next, armed with strategies to maintain momentum even when energy wanes.

Your journey continues with new tools at your disposal.

But your journey through "The Power of 24 Hours" is far from over. As you turn the page, you'll dive into "THE ART OF TIME MASTERY," where you'll refine your skills even further. This crucial chapter will introduce you to the TIME Mastery Framework, providing you with powerful tools to optimize every moment of your day.

A new adventure awaits to test your skills.

After mastering the concepts in "THE ART OF TIME MASTERY," you'll be prepared for your next thrilling adventure: "The Canyon of Quick Conquests." This immersive experience will bring the TIME Mastery Framework to life in vivid, sometimes unexpected ways.

You'll learn to:

- Track and identify where your time truly goes
- Investigate the patterns that shape your productivity

- **M**ap out the motives behind your actions
- **E**xecute strategies to make every moment count

This next adventure will bring the TIME Mastery Framework to life in vivid, sometimes unexpected ways. You'll navigate obstacles that mirror real-life time wasters, face decision points that reflect daily prioritization challenges, and seize opportunities that test your efficiency.

Are you ready to expand your mastery of time? Turn the page to begin the next chapter of your journey.

THE ART OF TIME MASTERY

"In the currency of time, every moment conserved is a precious asset, propelling you closer to achieving your goals."

As you descend from the Summit of Sustained Success, the lessons of the THRIVE framework still fresh in your mind, you realize that maintaining midday momentum is just one piece of the puzzle. To truly master your 24 hours, you need to refine your approach to time itself. Welcome to THE ART OF TIME MASTERY, where you'll learn to paint your days with purpose and precision.

In this chapter, we delve into the art of mastering your time. It's not just about managing your schedule; it's about enriching every minute of your day. Here, you'll learn to fine-tune your approach to time, leading a life marked by purpose and intentionality. We'll show you how to blend awareness, deliberate action, and strategic planning to transform even the simplest tasks into steps towards your bigger objectives. This is about turning routine into opportunities for growth and making the most out of each precious second.

The Essence of TIME Mastery

Imagine TIME Mastery as an intricate dance with the hours of your day. It means intimately knowing your rhythm—your strengths, challenges, and patterns—and moving in perfect sync with life's tempo. It's about aligning your daily actions with your ultimate goals, ensuring that each moment is meaningful and propels you forward.

Let's dive into how you can harness the TIME MASTERY framework to keep your momentum soaring through the afternoon slump and beyond.

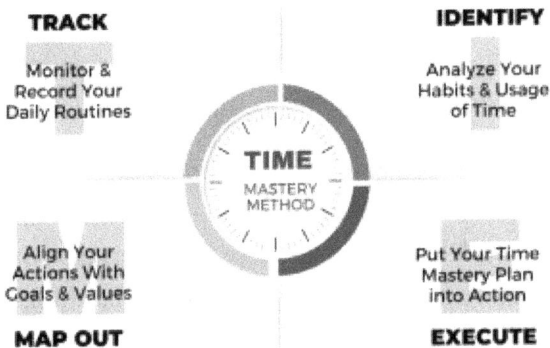

TRACK
Monitor &
Record Your
Daily Routines

IDENTIFY
Analyze Your
Habits & Usage
of Time

TIME
MASTERY
METHOD

Align Your
Actions With
Goals & Values

Put Your Time
Mastery Plan
into Action

MAP OUT

EXECUTE

The TIME Mastery Method:

To help you master your time and maximize your productivity, let's introduce each part of the TIME Mastery Method:

1. Track and Identify: Monitor and record your daily routines
2. Identify Patterns: Analyze your habits and time usage
3. Map Out Motives: Align your actions with your goals and values
4. Execute Strategies: Put your time mastery plan into action

As you explore each component of the TIME framework, consider: How might these techniques be put to the test in a high-stakes, time-sensitive scenario?

What challenges await in the Canyon of Quick Conquests?

Now let's break down each component of the TIME Mastery Framework:

T – TRACK & IDENTIFY

Let's kick off your TIME Mastery journey by getting real with how your day unfolds, moment by moment. This step is all about laying the groundwork for a crystal-clear view of your daily routines and pinpointing where your time actually slips away.

Here's the deal: You're going to become the keen observer of your own life. Jot down everything you do – yes, everything. From that big project at work to the quick coffee break, from scrolling through your phone to those moments of brainstorming. Nothing's too small to note.

As you meticulously log your activities, you might experience a moment of clarity—realizing that awareness is the first step to change. This insight can be transformative, shifting how you perceive and value each moment of your day.

Let's break it down:

1. **Tool Selection:** Choose a tracking method that seamlessly fits into your day. Whether it's a trusty notebook or a sleek app, consistency is key.
2. **Meticulous Logging:** Aim to record activities as they happen, or at least summarize each hour. This creates an accurate snapshot of your day.
3. **Categorization:** Group your activities as you go: work, personal time, leisure, distractions. This organization will be crucial when you analyze your time use later.
4. **Objectivity Check:** Remember, this isn't about self-judgment. You're here to gain clarity and understand patterns, not to criticize your choices.
5. **Comprehensive Coverage:** Don't leave anything out. Even small activities can reveal important insights about your time use.

Exercise: For one week, commit to tracking your time in 30-minute intervals. Use whatever method works best for you – a notebook, spreadsheet, or time-tracking app. Each day, spend 5 minutes reviewing and categorizing your activities.

Reflection:

- What surprises emerged about your time use?
- Which activities consumed more time than you anticipated?
- What patterns did you notice in how you spend your time?

This honest look at your day is your first step towards shaking off time-wasters and boosting your efficiency. By the end of this phase, you'll have a comprehensive map of where your time goes, setting the stage for some serious, informed improvements.

Remember, tracking isn't about perfection – it's about awareness. Even if you miss logging a few activities, you're still gaining valuable insights into your time use patterns.

I – IDENTIFY Patterns of Habit

Now that you've amassed a wealth of data about your daily activities, it's time to dig deeper. Even if you miss logging in a few activities, you're still gaining valuable insights into your time use. This phase is all about sharpening your understanding of how you really spend your hours.

Let's put on that detective hat and scrutinize your daily and weekly habits. Are there trends hiding in plain sight? Perhaps you veer off course at certain hours, or your energy takes a nosedive mid-afternoon. This step is about mapping the peaks and valleys of your day, identifying what fuels you and what leaves you drained.

While uncovering your productivity patterns, you might notice ripple effects in other areas of your life.

How might improving your work patterns impact your personal relationships or health habits?

Here's how to conduct your investigation:

1. **Peak Performance Periods:** Identify times when you consistently accomplish more. Are you a morning powerhouse or an afternoon achiever?

2. **Time-Waster Watch:** Be brutally honest. Where is time slipping through your fingers? Those "quick" social media checks that turn into scrolling marathons? Or maybe it's those meetings that seem to stretch endlessly?

3. **Energy Ebbs and Flows:** Note when you feel most energized and when you tend to slump. This isn't just about productivity; it's about understanding your overall energy patterns throughout the day.

4. **Task Type Analysis:** Which kinds of tasks do you gravitate towards at different times? Perhaps creative work flows best in the morning, while administrative tasks are your afternoon forte.

5. **Interruption Inventory:** Are there specific times when disruptions are more likely? This could be colleague check-ins, notification floods, or other external factors.

You're essentially decoding the story of your day. Which tasks ignite your passion, and which ones feel like a slog? Is there a particular time when procrastination's siren song becomes irresistible? Getting a grip on these patterns is crucial for crafting a day that truly resonates with your natural rhythms.

Exercise: Create a "Time Heat Map" of your week by using colors to represent different types of activities or energy levels. For example, use green for high productivity, yellow for moderate productivity, and red for low productivity or time-wasting activities. This visual representation can help you find patterns you might have overlooked.

Reflection:

- What was the most surprising pattern you uncovered?
- Can you pinpoint your "golden hours" – those times when you're at your most productive and focused?
- What are your biggest time-wasters, and when do they typically occur?
- How do your energy levels fluctuate throughout the day, and how does this align with your current schedule?

As you unearth these patterns, you might start to see opportunities for transformative change. Perhaps you'll realize that tackling your most challenging tasks during your peak productivity hours could dramatically boost your efficiency. Or maybe you'll recognize that strategic breaks during your typical slump times could help you recharge and finish the day strong.

By thoroughly investigating your habits, you're setting the stage for meaningful and lasting improvements in your daily routines. This deep understanding of your patterns is the foundation for mastering your time and crafting days that are not just productive, but deeply satisfying.

M – MAP OUT Your Motive

Uncover the 'why' behind your time usage. Are you investing in activities that truly matter, or are you being pulled off course by distractions or hidden fears?

Become a detective of your own behavior. Ask yourself:

- Why am I avoiding certain tasks?
- What makes me deeply engaged in others?

Understanding your motivations can guide you when faced with tough decisions or competing priorities. Consider:

- Purpose: Which activities align with your long-term goals and values?
- Passion: What tasks energize you? Why?
- Fears: What tasks do you avoid? What's holding you back?
- Values: Do your time-consuming activities align with your values?
- Energy: Which activities drain you, and which invigorate you?

This self-knowledge is your compass for mastering your time and making choices that truly matter to you.

Take a moment to reflect on what truly motivates you at your core. Is it the satisfaction of completing tasks, the pursuit of a grander vision, or the intrinsic joy of the work itself? Pinpointing your deepest motivators is essential for effective time mastery.

Reflection:

- What unexpected insights have you gained about your motivations?
- Are there activities in your routine that stem from fear or obligation rather than genuine interest or necessity?
- How can you better align your daily schedule with your authentic motivations and core values?

This step goes beyond improving time management; it's about aligning your daily life with your core values and motivations. By understanding why you do what you do, you can focus your time on what truly matters, making each day not only more productive but also deeply fulfilling.

Remember, time mastery comes from aligning your actions with your authentic self. As you map out your motives, you're not just organizing your schedule – you're crafting a life that resonates with your deepest aspirations and values.

E - Execute Your Insights into Action

Now it's time to roll up your sleeves and put your newfound knowledge to work. This crucial step is all about transforming those hard-earned insights into tangible results. It's where you bridge the gap between understanding and doing, taking those strategies you've crafted to combat your unique time-wasters and bringing them to life.

Let's break down how to make this happen:

1. **Prioritize by Motivation:** Use your Motivation Map to align tasks with your peak energy periods.
2. **Time-Block:** Schedule specific times for different task types to enhance focus and productivity.
3. **Two-Minute Rule:** Complete tasks that take less than two minutes immediately.
4. **Eisenhower Matrix:** Categorize tasks as urgent/important to focus on what truly matters.
5. **Pomodoro Technique:** Work in 25-minute focused sprints with short breaks.
6. **Distraction-Free Zone:** Design your workspace to minimize identified distractions.
7. **Power Hour:** Dedicate one hour daily to your most

challenging task during peak energy.

8. **One-Touch Rule:** Handle each item only once, dealing with it immediately.

Practical Application Tips:

- For procrastination-prone tasks: The Pomodoro Technique can make daunting projects feel more approachable.
- For energy slumps: Schedule your most engaging or crucial tasks during your identified peak energy times.
- For time-wasters: Set strict time limits for potentially distracting activities like email checks or social media use.

Exercise: Strategy Implementation Plan

1. Select three strategies from the list above (or devise your own based on your insights).
2. For each strategy, document:

- The specific problem it addresses
- Your detailed implementation plan
- Your start date
- How you'll measure its success

1. Commit to trying each strategy for at least one full week.

Reflection:

- Which strategy are you most eager to implement and why?
- What potential roadblocks do you anticipate in executing these strategies?
- How can you ensure adherence to your new strategies, especially during busy periods?

Remember, execution is where theory meets reality. Knowing what to do is just the first step; the real magic happens when you put that knowledge into action. Be patient with yourself as you implement these changes. Forming new habits and breaking old ones takes time and persistence.

As you progress, pay close attention to how these new strategies impact your day. Are they streamlining your workflow? Are you accomplishing more? Do you feel a reduction in stress? Use these observations to continually refine your approach.

This phase is all about turning plans into action, step by step, day by day. You're not just managing time anymore; you're on the path to mastering it. Embrace this process of active implementation and watch as your productivity and satisfaction soar to new heights.

Your Journey to Mastering Time

As we conclude our exploration of the TIME Mastery Framework, remember that true mastery of your time is an ongoing journey of refinement and growth. This framework provides you with a robust system to continuously enhance your productivity and align your actions with your deepest values and long-term goals.

By Tracking your routines, investigating your patterns, mapping your motives, and executing targeted strategies, you've laid the groundwork for a more efficient and fulfilling life. But the true art of time mastery lies not just in implementing these strategies, but in adapting them as you evolve.

Let's create a Continuous Improvement Plan:

1. Identify one area where you've seen the most improvement through the TIME Mastery Framework.

2. Choose one area that still needs work.
3. For each, create a specific plan for the next month:

- For the improved area: How will you maintain and build on this success?
- For the area needing work: What new strategy or adjustment will you try?

Remember, transformation doesn't happen overnight. It's a process of continuous refinement and growth. Be patient with yourself, celebrate your progress, and stay committed to your goals.

As you move forward, you may find that your definition of time mastery evolves. It's not just about doing more in less time—it's about ensuring that your time is spent in alignment with your values and long-term objectives.

Balancing Productivity & Well-Being

Time mastery isn't just about efficiency; it's about doing what matters while maintaining your health and happiness. A study in the Journal of Occupational Health Psychology found that employees who maintained a good work-life balance were not only more productive but also reported higher job and life satisfaction.

Reflection: What recent time commitments do you regret making? How could you have respectfully declined using your newfound TIME Mastery skills?

Exercise: Try a 5-minute mindfulness meditation daily for two weeks. Note any changes in your ability to Track your time use and investigate your patterns.

Overcoming TIME Mastery Obstacles

Even with the best intentions, we all face challenges in our quest for time mastery.

Let's address some common obstacles:

- **Tracking Troubles:** If you struggle with consistent time tracking, try setting regular reminders or linking the habit to an existing routine.
- **Investigation Inertia:** If analyzing your patterns feels overwhelming, start small. Focus on investigating just one aspect of your day at a time.
- **Motive Misalignment:** If you find it hard to connect with your true motives, try journaling or talking with a trusted friend to gain clarity.
- **Execution Roadblocks:** If implementing changes proves to be difficult, break your strategies into smaller, more manageable steps.

Reflection: Which aspect of the TIME Mastery Framework do you struggle with most? How can you apply the framework itself to overcome this challenge?

As we conclude this chapter on TIME Mastery, remember that mastering your time is an ongoing journey. The TIME Mastery Framework provides you with a robust system to continuously improve your productivity and align your actions with your deepest values and long-term goals.

Stay curious about your relationship with time. Regularly revisit the exercises and reflections in this chapter, using them as touchstones to gauge your progress and find new areas for improvement. Remember, the goal isn't perfection, but consistent growth and alignment with what truly matters to you.

Now, armed with these powerful tools and insights, you're ready to put your newfound TIME Mastery skills to the test. In our next adventure, "The Canyon of Quick Conquests," you'll face a series of challenges that will push your time management abilities to their limits.

Imagine standing at the edge of a vast canyon, where each path and crevice represents a different aspect of time mastery. As you navigate this rugged terrain, you'll encounter obstacles that mirror real-life time wasters, decision points that reflect daily prioritization challenges, and opportunities that test your ability to seize the moment efficiently.

This journey through the canyon will bring the TIME Mastery Framework to life in vivid, sometimes unexpected ways. It will challenge you to apply your skills in a dynamic environment, helping you internalize these strategies and make them second nature.

Are you ready to step into the Canyon of Quick Conquests and prove your mastery over time? Turn the page to begin this thrilling adventure, where every second counts and TIME Mastery is the key to reaching the summit of success.

The Maze of Quick Conquests

———

As lunchtime wraps you in the peaceful ambiance of a quaint café, you find yourself lost in thought, mulling over the profound insights from "The Art of Time Mastery" chapter. The principles of the TIME Framework echo in your mind, each element a key to unlocking a more purposeful and productive life.

You consider how these concepts might reshape your daily routine. "How would my day look if I truly mastered the art of tracking my time?" you wonder. "What hidden patterns might I uncover if I investigated my habits more closely?"

As these questions swirl in your mind, the café's gentle bustle fades into the background. Your gaze, fixed on the page but seeing beyond it, becomes a gateway to a vivid inner landscape.

A new adventure awaits to test your skills.

Suddenly, you're no longer in the quiet café. The world around you transforms, and you find yourself standing at the heart of a bustling metropolis. This is no ordinary city—it's a living, breathing manifestation of your daily life and the challenges you face in managing your time.

Skyscrapers loom overhead, their gleaming windows reflecting the countless tasks and responsibilities vying for your attention. The streets pulse with the energy of a thousand potential distractions, each one a test of your newfound time mastery skills.

You recognize the start of a new challenge.

You realize you've entered the Canyon of Quick Conquests, an urban maze that embodies the relentless pace of modern life and the myriad time management challenges you encounter each day. The city's rhythm, with its ebbs and flows, mirrors the dynamic nature of your own schedule, highlighting the critical importance of moving through time with intention and purpose.

As you take your first steps into this metaphorical landscape, you feel both excitement and apprehension. This journey through the city will be your proving ground, a chance to apply the wisdom of the TIME Framework in a visceral, immediate way.

The continual buzz of activity around you—car horns honking, conversations overlapping, the steady hum of urban life—represents the constant distractions that threaten to derail your focus and efficiency. Yet armed with your new knowledge, you feel prepared to navigate this complex terrain.

You center yourself, ready to face the challenge.

You take a deep breath, centering yourself amidst the urban chaos. It's time to put theory into practice, to transform your understanding of time mastery into real-world results. With determination in your steps, you begin your journey through the Canyon of Quick Conquests, ready to face whatever challenges this adventure may bring.

The 'Track and Identify' phase begins.

As you step deeper into the urban maze, the "Track and Identify" section of the TIME Framework springs to life around you. Each street and alley becomes a task or activity in your daily routine, challenging you to scrutinize how you navigate your day.

A moment of reflection reveals key questions.

You pause at an intersection, the cacophony of city life momentarily fading as you reflect, "Am I using my time wisely? Are these activities moving me closer to my goals, or are they just distractions?" The question echoes off the towering buildings, forcing you to confront the reality of your choices.

Every turn represents a decision in your daily life.

Every turn you make in this concrete jungle parallels a decision in your daily life. Some paths lead to wide, sunlit avenues of productivity, while others twist into narrow, shadowy alleys of wasted time. You realize that mapping your route through this maze is akin to charting the course of your day, each choice carrying the weight of potential progress or stagnation.

The challenge becomes clear: to honestly assess your current time usage amidst the urban chaos. You must discern which activities are merely keeping you busy and which are truly effective in propelling you towards your goals. As you navigate this section of the city, you're not just finding your way through physical streets but mentally mapping out a more efficient approach to your daily life.

Patterns in your behavior emerge from the urban landscape.

Gradually, patterns in your behavior emerge like the winding streets of the city. Could that circular path you keep taking be the digital equivalent of checking your email every five minutes? Is that dead-end alley a metaphor for the endless scroll of social media that eats away at your productive hours? Each realization is a key that unlocks a door to more effective time management, the city itself becoming your guide.

This growing awareness marks a transition. You're moving from simple recognition of your habits to a deeper understanding of their impact on your life. As you round a corner, the cityscape shifts subtly, signaling your entry into the 'Investigate Patterns' phase of your journey. Here, the urban landscape promises to reveal not just the what of your time usage, but the why, inviting you to delve deeper into the triggers and consequences of your daily routines.

You feel yourself aligning with your broader aspirations.

With each step, you feel yourself aligning more closely with your broader aspirations, the city's rhythm now pulsing in sync with your own goals and values. The maze of modern efficiency stretches before you, ready to unveil more secrets of effective time management.

As you delve deeper into the urban maze, the 'Investigate Patterns' phase of your journey unfolds. The city's rhythm begins to reveal itself, each recurring route and routine mirroring the habits in your daily life.

You find yourself automatically turning down a familiar street, much like your habit of checking emails first thing in the morning. This realization prompts you to question, "Why do I always prioritize this task, even when it's not the most urgent?" The bustling avenue of constant communication suddenly seems less essential, more a distraction from your main objectives.

As you navigate the complex grid of streets, you start to grasp the deeper reasons behind your habits. "Am I choosing this path just to feel busy, or is it actually moving me closer to my goals?" This introspection shifts your focus from merely what you do to why you do it, a pivotal moment in your journey through the urban landscape.

Walking deeper into the urban maze, the 'Investigate Patterns' phase of your journey unfolds. The city's rhythm begins to reveal itself, each recurring route and routine mirroring the habits in your daily life.

You find yourself automatically turning down a familiar street, much like your habit of checking emails first thing in the morning. This realization prompts you to question, "Why do I always prioritize this task, even when it's not the most urgent?" The bustling avenue of constant communication suddenly seems less essential, more a distraction from your main objectives.

Deeper motivations come into focus.

As you navigate the complex grid of streets, you start to grasp the deeper reasons behind your habits. "Am I choosing this path just to feel busy, or is it actually moving me closer to my goals?" This introspection shifts your focus from merely what you do to why you do it, a pivotal moment in your journey through the urban landscape.

The challenge of scrutinizing habits intensifies.

The 'Investigate Patterns' challenge involves scrutinizing these habitual routes. You realize that if your morning email check is simply a way to ease into your day, perhaps there's a more direct path to your goals - a more invigorating route to start your daily journey.

As you gain these insights, the cityscape subtly shifts, signaling your transition to the 'Motive Understanding' phase. The urban environment transforms, presenting you with landmarks and monuments that symbolize your various motivations.

Reflection reveals true priorities.

You pause before a grand statue, contemplating, "Does this represent a true passion, or merely an attempt to stay busy?" This internal dialogue helps you distinguish between actions that genuinely further your long-term goals and those that simply fill time.

The challenge intensifies as you navigate between towering skyscrapers of urgent tasks and serene parks of important but less pressing activities. You acknowledge, "I've been prioritizing the urgent over the truly important, neglecting what genuinely matters." This realization guides you to choose paths that align more closely with your core values and long-term objectives.

A sense of harmony emerges from understanding motives.

Mastering the 'Motive Understanding' challenge brings a sense of harmony between your daily journey through the city and your ultimate destination. With this clarity, you enter the final phase: 'Execute Strategies.'

In this stage, the city transforms into an obstacle course of daily tasks and challenges. Each hurdle represents a real-life task, and your method of overcoming these obstacles mirrors how you should manage your time.

As you deftly navigate this urban assault course, you think, "I need to be proactive, not just reactive. Anticipation and preparation are key." This insight sharpens your focus, enhancing your ability to prioritize and avoid distractions.

Confidence surges as you master the framework.

Successfully moving through this final phase, you feel a surge of confidence. You've translated the insights from the TIME Framework into actionable steps, ready to implement in your daily life.

Reality shifts back, but lessons remain.

As you emerge from the final twists and turns of the Maze of Quick Conquests, you find yourself back in the quiet café. The bustling city fades, but the lessons remain vivid in your mind. The strategies and insights you've gathered offer a concrete guide for revamping your daily schedule.

Armed with the TIME Framework and a deepened understanding of personal productivity, you feel prepared to face the rest of your day - and indeed, all your days - with renewed assurance and a strategic approach. You've learned to navigate the labyrinth of tasks and distractions, emerging with a clearer sense of purpose and efficiency.

But as you reflect on your journey through the maze, a new challenge begins to take shape in your mind. You realize that mastering your time isn't just about managing what you do - it's also about what you choose not to do. The power of decisively declining tasks, invitations, and distractions that don't align with your goals begins to dawn on you.

The next chapter beckons with new insights.

The next chapter, "The Power of Saying No," beckons, offering the tantalizing prospect of further refining your mastery over time.

You begin to wonder: How will you navigate the delicate balance between seizing opportunities and protecting your time? What strategies will you develop to say 'no' gracefully yet firmly? How might mastering the art of refusal transform your productivity and well-being?

With these questions swirling in your mind, you prepare to turn the page. The Maze of Quick Conquests has sharpened your time management skills, but the true test lies ahead in mastering the art of refusal. Are you ready to dive into "The Power of Saying No" and unlock a new level of control over your time and energy?

The journey continues, with greater challenges ahead.

Your fingers hover over the page, poised to embark on this next crucial stage of your journey. The power to shape your day - and your life - through strategic refusal awaits. And beyond this chapter, you know an even greater challenge looms: The Desert of Decisive Denial, where you'll put your newfound knowledge to the ultimate test.

Turn the page when you're ready to explore the transformative power of 'no' and prepare yourself for the adventures that lie ahead.

THE POWER OF SAYING NO

———

"Sometimes in life, saying 'no' is like hitting the pause button, making sure your priorities and your time stay aligned."

After mastering the TIME TACKLE system and journeying through "The Canyon of Quick Conquests," you've gained valuable insights into optimizing your day and identifying what truly matters. This progress brings us to a pivotal concept that further enhances the art of efficiency: the power of saying 'no.'

As you begin this chapter, reflect on your journey through the Maze of Quick Conquests.

How will this new skill transform your ability to navigate life's challenges?

In today's fast-paced world, we're conditioned to say "yes" reflexively, constantly striving to seize every opportunity. However, the true path to success often lies in the strategic art of refusal. Embracing the power of "no" isn't about shutting down possibilities; it's about intentionally curating your time and energy.

By prioritizing what truly matters, you protect your time, preserve your well-being, and maintain healthy boundaries. It's a powerful tool that complements your efficiency and prioritization skills, leading you toward a more fulfilling and focused life.

Why 'No' Matters

Saying 'no' does more than just free up your time; it's a crucial aspect of self-care and boundary-setting. It helps prevent burnout by ensuring you're not overextending yourself. It allows you to focus deeply on the tasks that are truly important, enhancing both the quality of your work and your satisfaction with it. Additionally, saying 'no' can foster respect from others; it signals that you value your time and are serious about your commitments.

Consider the ripple effect of each 'yes' in your life. Every commitment you make not only occupies time but also mental and emotional energy. By mastering the art of saying 'no,' you're not just protecting your schedule – you're safeguarding your overall well-being and capacity to excel in what truly matters.

The Art of Refusal

Mastering the art of saying 'no' involves more than just uttering the word. It's about communicating your refusal clearly, respectfully, and aligned with your values.

Here are some strategies to refine this skill:

1. **Understand Your Why:** Before you can comfortably say 'no,' you need to be clear on why you're doing it. Is the request in conflict with your priorities? Does it clash with your schedule or energy levels? Understanding your reasons will make it easier to communicate your decision.

2. **Communicate Clearly and Compassionately:** Be direct but kind in your refusal. You don't need to offer a lengthy explanation, but a simple, honest reason can help the other person understand your decision.

3. **Offer Alternatives:** When possible, suggest other solutions or alternatives. If you can't take on a request, maybe you know someone who can, or perhaps you could tackle the request at

a later date.

4. **Practice:** Saying 'no' can be challenging at first, especially if you're used to saying 'yes' to everything. Like any skill, it gets easier with practice. Start with small refusals and build up to bigger ones.

The Psychology of 'No':

Understanding the psychological impact of saying 'no' can be empowering. Research in social psychology suggests that people respect those who can set clear boundaries. By saying 'no,' you're not just managing your time; you're also shaping how others perceive and interact with you. This awareness can help overcome the fear of negative consequences often associated with refusal.

Exercise: Role-play saying 'no' to common requests. Write down five scenarios where you often struggle to say 'no.' For each, craft a respectful refusal. Practice saying these out loud, paying attention to your tone and body language.

The Psychological Barriers to 'No'

Understanding the fears that hold us back from saying 'no' is crucial. Common barriers include:

1. **Fear of Disappointing Others:** We often say 'yes' to avoid letting people down. Remember, short-term disappointment is better than long-term resentment.
2. **Fear of Missing Out (FOMO):** Sometimes we say 'yes' because we're afraid of missing an opportunity. Trust that by saying 'no' to less important things, you're saying 'yes' to what truly matters.
3. **Need for Approval:** The desire to be liked can drive us to overcommit. Recognize that respect often comes from setting

clear boundaries.

Reflection: Identify which of these fears resonates most with you. How has it impacted your ability to say 'no' in the past? How might overcoming this fear change your life?

Cultural and Professional Factors

The ability to say 'no' can be perceived differently across cultures and professional settings. In some contexts, direct refusal might be seen as rude, while in others, it's respected as clear communication.

Exercise: Research how 'no' is communicated in different cultures or industries. How can you adapt your approach to saying 'no' in various contexts while still maintaining your boundaries?

Building the 'No' Muscle

Developing the habit of saying 'no' is like building muscle—it takes consistent exercise and time.

Here's a long-term strategy:

1. **Start Small:** Begin with low-stakes situations where saying 'no' feels less daunting.
2. **Reflect and Adjust:** After each 'no,' reflect on how it felt and the outcome. What worked well? What could you improve?
3. **Gradually Increase Difficulty:** As you become more comfortable, practice saying 'no' in more challenging situations.
4. **Celebrate Your Successes:** Acknowledge each time you successfully set a boundary. This positive reinforcement will help solidify the habit.

Visualization Exercise: Before facing a situation where you might need to say 'no,' take a moment to visualize yourself confidently and kindly refusing. Imagine the sense of relief and empowerment that follows. This mental rehearsal can make the actual moment of saying 'no' feel more natural and less daunting.

30-Day Challenge: For the next 30 days, embark on a transformative journey to harness the power of 'no':

1. **Week 1 - The Gentle 'No':** Say 'no' to one small, non-essential request.
2. **Week 2 - The Firm 'No':** Decline a more significant commitment that doesn't align with your goals.
3. **Week 3 - The Redirecting 'No':** Refuse a request while offering an alternative solution.
4. **Week 4 - The Self-Care 'No':** Turn down an invitation or task to prioritize your well-being.

Throughout this challenge, maintain a 'No' Power Journal. After each refusal, record:

- The situation and your response
- Your emotional state before and after
- Any unexpected outcomes or insights

At the end of each week, reflect on how your comfort with saying 'no' has evolved. Notice any changes in your productivity, stress levels, and overall satisfaction.

This challenge isn't just about saying 'no' more often—it's about saying 'yes' to what truly matters in your life. Are you ready to unlock the transformative power of strategic refusal?

Balancing 'No' with Opportunity

While saying 'no' is essential for maintaining focus and well-being, it's equally important to balance it with openness to opportunities that align with your goals and values. This balance ensures that you're not just guarding your time against unwanted demands but also nurturing growth and progression in areas that matter most to you.

Exercise: Create a decision-making framework for evaluating opportunities. Include criteria such as alignment with goals, required time investment, potential impact, and personal interest.

Use this framework to practice making quick, informed decisions about whether to say 'yes' or 'no' to future requests.

Remember, the power of saying 'no' isn't about closing doors; it's about opening up space for what truly enriches your life, ensuring that you're not just busy, but meaningfully engaged with tasks and relationships that matter.

As we conclude this chapter, reflect on how mastering the art of 'no' can transform your daily life. In our next adventure, "The Desert of Decisive Denial," you'll have the opportunity to put these concepts into practice in a challenging environment. Prepare to navigate the mirages of temptation and the dunes of distraction, where every 'no' brings you closer to your true oasis of productivity and fulfillment.

As you prepare for your journey through the Desert of Decisive Denial, consider how the principles you've learned here will be put to the test.

How will you discern between mirages of distraction and true oases of opportunity? The skills you're developing now will be your compass in that challenging terrain.

Are you ready to harness the power of 'no' and take control of your time and energy? Turn the page when you're prepared to embark on this transformative journey through the Desert of Decisive Denial.

The Desert of Decisive Denial

───

R ush hour transforms into a landscape of decisions.
As you navigate the congested afternoon traffic, the lessons from "The Power of Saying No" echo in your mind. Suddenly, the busy intersection before you shimmers. The sea of vehicles morphs into sand dunes, and the traffic lights become distant mirages. You find yourself at the wheel, no longer just driving home, but steering through the vast Desert of Decisive Denial.

Your car becomes your guide through the sands of choice.

Your car glides over the sand as smoothly as it did on asphalt, the transition so seamless you barely notice the change in terrain. The tires, once suited for city streets, now seem perfectly adapted to the desert landscape, gripping the shifting sands with surprising ease. The familiar purr of the engine takes on a new cadence, harmonizing with the rhythm of your thoughts and the ebb and flow of the dunes.

The dashboard flickers, its digital display shimmering like a mirage before settling into a new configuration. Gone are the familiar gauges of speed and fuel. In their place, a series of colorful bars and charts materialize, displaying abstract yet somehow intuitive measures of your inner state. A pulsing blue line shows your current energy levels, fluctuating with each consideration of a new opportunity. A pie chart breaks down your priorities, its sections expanding and contracting as you weigh different options against your life goals.

The landscape mirrors your decision-making process.

The desert landscape spreads out before you, each feature reflecting your choices in life. Small, gentle dunes represent easy, everyday decisions you barely think about - like what to have for lunch. You cruise over these with hardly a bump.

Bigger dunes appear in the distance. These stand for more important choices, like job changes or big commitments. They require you to slow down and think carefully about how to approach them. Your car works harder to climb these, just like how big decisions take more effort to make.

Sometimes, you see enormous dunes that seem to touch the sky. These are the large, life-changing decisions. You might need to stop and plan before tackling these, knowing that what you see from the top could change everything.

Between the dunes are flat, open areas. These are the calm periods in life when you're not facing many big choices. But you stay alert, watching for unexpected challenges or opportunities that might pop up.

The whole desert stretches as far as you can see in every direction. Each way you could go offers different challenges and rewards. The path you choose to drive will create your own unique trail across this sea of decisions.

The pressure to say 'yes' looms overhead.

The hot desert sun beats down on you from above. It's not just hot; it feels like it's pushing on you. This heat is like the pressure you feel to say yes to everything people ask of you. Just as the sun makes you sweat, always saying yes can make you feel stressed and tired.

Far away, you see something that looks like a peaceful, cool spot with water and shade. This is like the calm feeling you could have if you learn to say no sometimes. It looks so nice, but it seems far away and hard to reach.

Mirage 1: The Helpful Volunteer

The first mirage appears on your path.

As you drive up and over a big sand hill, you hear a 'ding' from your car's GPS. It's telling you about a new way you could go. The GPS says, "New route available: Community Project Leadership."

Then, you see a picture seeming to float in the air in front of you. This picture shows you leading a group of people, making new friends, and learning new things. It looks exciting and like it could be good for you. But remember, in the desert, sometimes things you see are not real - they're just tricks of the light called mirages.

You pause to evaluate the opportunity.

You slow your car down and pull over to a spot where you can see all around you. It's like taking a moment to think before you make a big decision. You take a deep breath and ask yourself some important questions:

1. Does this new opportunity fit with where you're already trying to go in life?
2. Do you have enough energy to do this new thing, or are you already tired from what you're doing now?
3. If you choose to do this new thing, what other important stuff might you have to give up?
4. Are you excited about where this new opportunity could lead, or do you just like the idea of trying something different?

Mirage 2: The Extra Work Project

The second mirage tests your work-life balance.

Just as you start driving again, your work phone makes a noise. It's someone from your job calling about a new, urgent project. They make it sound really important, like it could help your career a lot. As they talk, you feel like the sand under your car is moving, trying to pull you in a new direction. It's like feeling pressure to say yes to more work, even if you're already busy.

You navigate the mirage with newfound skills.

You hold onto the steering wheel tightly, remembering what you've learned about making good choices. You think carefully about:

1. Is this really as urgent as they say, or did someone just not plan well?
2. If you say yes to this, will it make it hard to finish the work you've already promised to do?
3. Does this fit with what you want for your career in the long run?

A social temptation appears on the horizon.

As you drive on, you see what looks like a big sign in the distance. It's showing a picture of a fun party with all your friends. Seeing this makes you feel a mix of happy and sad. You want to see your friends, but you also have other important things to do. It's like trying to figure out how to have time for fun and still get everything else done.

Mirage 3: The Social Gathering

As you crest another dune, a beam of light suddenly appears, projecting an image in the air before you. It's as if someone set up an invisible screen in the middle of the desert. The projection shows a lively gathering of your friends and family. You see smiling faces, hear echoes of laughter, and almost smell the delicious food being shared.

A voice whispers on the wind, "Life is short. Don't miss out on these precious moments with loved ones."

This vivid mirage makes you pause and consider your social connections:

1. When was the last time you spent quality time with friends and family?
2. How would attending this gathering make you feel - energized or drained?
3. Is there a way to maintain these relationships without neglecting other responsibilities?
4. Could strengthening these social bonds actually improve other areas of your life?

The projection looks so real and inviting, you could almost step into it. But you remember that in this desert of decisions, not everything is as it appears. You need to decide if this is a genuine opportunity for meaningful connection, or if it's a mirage that might lead you off your intended path.

As you contemplate this choice, you feel the pull of social bonds tugging at your heart, challenging you to balance personal relationships with other life priorities.

Mirage 3: The Social Gathering

The next mirage materializes as a group of friends inviting you to a long-anticipated event. This challenges you to balance personal relationships with other life priorities.

You consider:

1. **Current commitments:** How does this align with existing responsibilities?
2. **Energy levels:** Will this event rejuvenate or deplete you?
3. **Relationship impact:** How might your decision affect your friendships?
4. **Work-life balance:** Are you maintaining a healthy equilibrium?
5. **FOMO:** Are you drawn to the event or anxious about missing out?

After navigating this mirage, you contemplate how you now approach balancing social commitments with personal and professional goals.

Mirage 4: The Side Hustle Offer

Deeper in the desert, you encounter an enthusiastic entrepreneur with a tantalizing new venture proposition. This mirage probes your entrepreneurial instincts and long-term vision.

You evaluate:

1. **Opportunity costs:** How would pursuing this opportunity impact your existing commitments, projects, or responsibilities? What would you need to sacrifice or put on hold?
2. **Capacity:** Do you currently have the time, energy, skills, and resources needed to take on this opportunity effectively? Will it stretch you too thin or lead to burnout?

3. **Market potential:** Is this a genuine opportunity with realistic potential for growth, profit, or personal development? Or is it a fleeting distraction that won't yield significant results?
4. **Risk tolerance:** What are the potential risks and uncertainties associated with this opportunity? Are you comfortable with the level of risk involved, and do you have contingency plans in place?
5. **Personal motivations:** What are your true motivations for pursuing this opportunity? Are you driven by genuine passion, curiosity, or a sense of purpose? Or are you motivated by external pressures, fear of missing out, or a desire for validation?

After making your decision, you reflect on how your ability to evaluate opportunities has evolved.

Mirage 5: The Family Request

The final mirage places you in a familiar setting, with a relative asking you to organize a large family reunion. This scenario delves into family dynamics and personal boundaries.

You consider:

1. **Current commitments:** Can you take this on without compromising other responsibilities?
2. **Emotional implications:** How might your decision affect family relationships?
3. **Expertise:** Are you truly the best fit, or is this based on family assumptions?
4. **Personal boundaries:** How do you balance family obligations with personal needs?
5. **Long-term impacts:** How might this influence future family

expectations?

As you navigate the final complex mirage, which combines elements of all previous challenges, you put into practice everything you've learned about the power of saying "no." With each decision, you feel your confidence growing, your boundaries strengthening.

Suddenly, the desert landscape begins to fade. The mirages dissolve, and the world around you slowly comes back into focus. You find yourself once again in your car, still stopped at the red light where your inner journey began. But something has changed – you have changed.

The ability to say 'no' is no longer just a concept, but a powerful tool integrated into your decision-making process. The challenges that once seemed overwhelming now feel manageable. You've learned to see through the illusions of urgency and obligation, focusing instead on what truly aligns with your goals and values.

As you sit there, hands on the steering wheel, you realize that each choice to decline a misaligned opportunity is a step towards a more fulfilling, purposeful existence. This inner journey through the Desert of Decisive Denial has strengthened your resolve, sharpened your decision-making skills, and reinforced the importance of boundary-setting.

You reflect on how far you've come in your journey through "The Power of 24 Hours." Your approach to time management and decision-making has evolved dramatically. You're no longer at the mercy of every request or opportunity; instead, you're the master of your time and energy.

Just then, the traffic light turns green – a fitting symbol for the path ahead now open before you. As you accelerate forward, you feel a renewed sense of purpose and clarity. You're eager to put these newfound skills into practice in your daily life, integrating the power of 'no' with the other strategies you've learned.

The adventure may be over, but your journey of growth continues. As you drive on, you look forward to exploring the next chapter, ready to see how these skills of decisiveness and boundary-setting will further enhance your mastery over the power of 24 hours.

CONNECT & UNWIND

———

"Evenings are the silent whispers of reflection, echoing the lessons of the day and preparing the symphony of tomorrow."

As you emerge from the Desert of Decisive Denial, having mastered the art of saying "no," you realize that protecting your time is only half the battle. Now, it's time to learn how to use that carefully guarded time to recharge and prepare for the challenges ahead. Welcome to CONNECT & UNWIND, where we'll explore the art of crafting evenings that not only help you recover from the day's demands but also set the stage for tomorrow's success.

The CONNECT framework offers a comprehensive approach to evening routines that extend beyond mere relaxation. It's about creating an evening that complements the day's energy with night-time tranquility, establishing a 24-hour cycle that supports both your productivity and your well-being.

By focusing on Connection, Observation, Nurturing, Nourishment, Exercise, Contemplation, and Thankfulness, the CONNECT framework provides a holistic approach to your evenings. It ensures that you not only unwind from the day's stresses but also strengthen relationships, engage in personal growth, and prepare yourself mentally and physically for the challenges ahead.

As we explore each element of CONNECT, you'll discover how to transform your evenings from a haphazard wind-down into a purposeful routine that enhances your overall quality of life. You'll learn to create a rhythm that aligns with your natural energy cycles, fostering a sense of balance and fulfillment that extends far beyond the evening hours.

The CONNECT & Unwind Routine

To help you master your evenings and prepare for restful nights, let's introduce each part of the CONNECT & Unwind Routine:

1. **C**onnect: Engage meaningfully with loved ones
2. **O**bserve: Practice mindfulness and self-awareness
3. **N**urture: Engage in activities that feed your soul
4. **N**ourish: Provide proper care for your body and mind
5. **E**xercise: Incorporate light physical activity
6. **C**ontemplate: Reflect on your day and set intentions
7. **T**hank: Practice gratitude for the day's experiences

Now let's break down each component of the CONNECT & Unwind Routine:

C – CONNECT with Loved Ones

After prioritizing and saying "no" throughout the day, it's crucial to reconnect with family and friends. This isn't just nice; it's necessary. Think about a moment when a loved one shared something profound with you - perhaps a child's innocent wisdom, a partner's vulnerability, or a friend's breakthrough. These are the moments that remind us why we strive for efficiency - to create space for genuine connections.

When we CONNECT in our evenings, we're not just unwinding; we're reinforcing the very foundations of our lives. We're creating space for those profound moments of insight that remind us of our values and what truly matters. We're fostering an environment where our loved ones can share their thoughts, dreams, and even their worries, knowing we're fully present to listen and support.

This connection time isn't a luxury - it's a necessity. It's what fuels us to face the next day with renewed purpose. It's what makes all our efforts to manage our time and increase our productivity meaningful. Consider your own life: What moments of connection stand out to you? How do these interactions shape your perspective and motivate you?

Remember, at the end of the day, the point of having more time is to spend it with the people who matter most. As you develop your evening routine, think about how you can create opportunities for these meaningful connections. Whether it's a family dinner, a heart-to-heart chat with a friend, or simply being present for your loved ones, these moments are the true measure of a day well spent.

O – OPTIMIZE Your Environment

Creating the right environment for your evening is like setting the stage for a performance—in this case, the performance of rest, relaxation, and renewal. This step is about transforming your space from a hub of daytime activity into a sanctuary of evening calm.

As you create your evening sanctuary, consider how this practice might serve as a buffer against life's storms. How might your optimized environment anchor you when challenges arise?

Here's how to create a space that nurtures relaxation and prepares you for restorative sleep:

1. **Tidy Up:** Clear away clutter to create visual calm.
2. **Adjust Lighting:** Use dim, warm lights to promote melatonin production.
3. **Set Temperature:** Keep the room cool (60-67°F/15-19°C) for better sleep.
4. **Create Comfort Zones:** Designate areas for evening activities.
5. **Engage Senses:** Use calming scents and sounds to promote relaxation.

N – NOURISH Your Body and Mind

In the hustle of daily life, it's easy to neglect the activities that truly feed our souls. This step is about reclaiming that vital time for personal growth and enjoyment. It's not just about relaxation; it's about engaging in activities that replenish your mental and emotional reserves, preparing you for the challenges and opportunities of tomorrow.

Think of this nourishment as essential fuel for your well-being. Just as your body needs nutritious food, your mind and spirit need enriching experiences to thrive. By dedicating time to these activities, you're investing in your overall health, creativity, and resilience.

These nourishing activities aren't just for calm evenings. They can be powerful tools when life gets turbulent. How might you adapt these practices to help you weather unexpected challenges?

1. **Read:** Enjoy a book for relaxation or knowledge.
2. **Journal:** Write down thoughts to process your day.
3. **Pursue Hobbies:** Engage in activities you love.
4. **Meditate:** Practice mindfulness to calm your mind.
5. **Move Gently:** Do light stretching or take a leisurely walk.
6. **Learn:** Dedicate time to acquiring new knowledge or skills.
7. **Create:** Express yourself through writing, drawing, or other mediums.

N – NAVIGATE Tomorrow

As the day ends, it's tempting to switch off completely. But taking a few moments to plan for tomorrow can boost your productivity and ease morning stress. This isn't about making a strict schedule—it's about setting intentions and priorities to guide your actions when you wake up.

Think of this process as charting a course for a journey. You're not planning every single step, but you're deciding on your destination and identifying the major landmarks along the way. This approach provides direction without stifling flexibility.

This forward-thinking approach isn't just for smooth sailing. It's a crucial skill for navigating life's storms. How might this practice help you stay on course when unexpected winds blow?

Here's how to navigate tomorrow effectively:

1. **Check Calendar:** Review upcoming commitments.
2. **Choose Your "Big Three":** Identify your three most important tasks.
3. **Set Your Intentions:** Decide on your approach and mindset for the day.
4. **Visualize Success:** Mentally rehearse navigating the day well.

5. **Anticipate Challenges:** Consider potential obstacles and solutions.

6. **Plan Your First Action:** Decide how you'll start your workday.

E – ENGAGE in Relaxation

After a day filled with activity, decisions, and potentially stress, engaging in relaxation is not just a luxury—it's a necessity. This step is about intentionally shifting your body and mind from a state of alertness to one of calm, paving the way for restful sleep and rejuvenation.

Think of relaxation as the bridge between your active day and your restful night. It's a time to let go of the day's tensions, quiet the mind's chatter, and prepare your body for the important work of sleep and recovery.

These relaxation techniques are more than just evening practices. They're lifelines you can grab onto when stress threatens to overwhelm you. How might you use these methods as stabilizing forces in turbulent times?

Here are some effective ways to engage in relaxation:

1. **Deep Breathing:** Use the 4-7-8 method to activate relaxation.
2. **Gentle Stretching:** Release tension with slow, focused movements.
3. **Meditation:** Practice brief, quiet focus or use a guided app.
4. **Progressive Muscle Relaxation:** Tense and relax each muscle group.
5. **Mindfulness:** Immerse in a calming activity using all senses.
6. **Visualization:** Imagine a peaceful scene in detail.

C – CULTIVATE Gratitude

In the rush of daily life, it's easy to focus on what went wrong or what's still left undone. However, taking time to cultivate gratitude can shift your perspective, ending your day on a positive note and setting the stage for a more optimistic tomorrow. This practice isn't about ignoring challenges; it's about recognizing the good that exists alongside them.

Gratitude is like a muscle—the more you exercise it, the stronger it becomes. Over time, this practice can rewire your brain to more readily notice and appreciate the positive aspects of your life.

Gratitude isn't just for good days. It can be a powerful force in challenging times, helping you find silver linings in the darkest clouds. How might this practice serve as a beacon of hope during life's storms?

Here are several ways to cultivate gratitude in your evening routine:

1. **Gratitude Journal:** Write three things you're grateful for daily.
2. **Gratitude Meditation:** Reflect quietly on things you're thankful for.
3. **Gratitude Jar:** Add written notes of gratitude to a jar nightly.
4. **Gratitude Letters:** Write weekly notes of appreciation to others.
5. **Sensory Gratitude:** Identify one grateful thing for each sense daily.
6. **Gratitude Reframe:** Find something positive in a daily challenge.

T – TRANSITION to Sleep

The final step in our CONNECT & RESTORE routine is crucial: the transition to sleep. This isn't merely about lying down and closing your eyes; it's about creating a consistent routine that signals to your body and mind that it's time to wind down and prepare for restorative sleep.

Think of this transition as a gentle descent into restfulness, rather than an abrupt shift from wakefulness to sleep. By setting up a consistent bedtime routine, you're essentially training your body to recognize sleep cues, making it easier to fall asleep and improve the quality of your rest.

A consistent sleep transition isn't just a fair-weather practice. It can be your anchor in stormy seas, providing stability when everything else feels chaotic. How might you adapt this routine to serve you even in unpredictable circumstances?

Here are key elements to include in your sleep transition routine:

1. **Consistent Schedule:** Set regular sleep and wake times.
2. **Wind-Down Time:** Begin routine 30-60 minutes before bed.
3. **Calming Activities:** Read, listen to soft music, or stretch.
4. **Dim Lighting:** Use soft, warm lights to promote melatonin.
5. **Cool Room:** Keep bedroom around 65°F (18°C).
6. **Comfort:** Ensure bed and bedding are comfortable.
7. **Avoid Stimulants:** Skip caffeine, alcohol, and heavy meals near bedtime.
8. **Limit Electronics:** Stop screen use 30 minutes before going to sleep.

Maintaining Long-Term Consistency

1. **Start Small:** Begin with a 15-minute evening routine and gradually extend it as it becomes habitual.
2. **Track Your Progress:** Use a habit-tracking app or journal to

monitor your consistency and the effects on your sleep and next-day productivity.

3. **Be Flexible:** Have a "minimum viable routine" for busy nights, ensuring you maintain some consistency even when time is tight.

4. **Regular Reviews:** Monthly, assess what's working and what isn't. Be willing to adjust your routine as your life circumstances change.

The Science of Evening Routines

Research has shown that consistent evening routines can significantly improve sleep quality and next-day performance. A study in the Journal of Sleep Research found that individuals with regular bedtime routines fell asleep faster and reported better sleep quality.

By embracing CONNECT & UNWIND, you're not just ending your day; you're enriching it. You're setting the foundation for a night that rejuvenates your mind, body, and spirit and preparing yourself for the potential and challenges of tomorrow. This chapter has guided you through developing an evening routine that revitalizes your energy, sharpens your focus, and balances your life, ensuring you're ready to seize each day with vigor and purpose.

As we conclude this chapter on CONNECT & UNWIND, reflect on how these practices can transform your evenings into a powerful launchpad for daily success. Each element of the CONNECT framework offers not just a way to end your day, but a tool to fortify yourself against life's challenges.

The journey to mastering the power of your 24 hours continues, and your evening routine will play a crucial role. In our next adventure, 'The Storm of Strategic Strength,' you'll have the opportunity to put these concepts into practice in a dynamic and challenging environment. How will your carefully crafted routine weather the tempests of daily life? How will you maintain your evening sanctuary when external forces threaten to disrupt your calm?

Prepare to navigate the unpredictable waters ahead, using your evening routine as an anchor of stability and renewal. Turn the page when you're ready to discover the true power of a well-crafted evening routine in the face of life's storms.

The Twilight of Connection

As evening settles in, you find yourself reflecting on the lessons from the "CONNECT & UNWIND" chapter. The weight of the day begins to lift as you contemplate how to put these new concepts into practice.

Reality shifts, revealing a serene lakeside scene.

Suddenly, your surroundings shift, and you're transported to the edge of a serene lake. The water, smooth as glass, mirrors the vibrant hues of the sunset, symbolizing the transition from the busy day to a peaceful evening.

A mysterious journey begins at twilight.

This lakeside scene isn't just a change of scenery; it's a living representation of the CONNECT framework, inviting you to experience each element in this tranquil setting. As you begin your journey, you notice a glint of something partially buried in the sand near the water's edge. Curiosity piqued, you wonder: How will this evening adventure prepare you for the challenges that lie ahead?

Warm conversations spark meaningful connections.

C - Connect: Your lakeside stroll leads you to small groups gathered around cozy campfires. Their laughter and warm conversations remind you of the importance of connecting with loved ones. As you approach, you overhear snippets of conversation about a local legend - a mysterious message in a bottle that appears to those seeking balance and purpose in their lives. You feel a gentle nudge to reach out to someone important in your life, reinforcing the value of meaningful connections in your evening routine. How might these connections serve as anchors in stormy times, and perhaps help you unravel the mystery that seems to be unfolding?

Nature grounds you in the present moment.

O - Observe: Pausing by the water's edge, you decide to remove your shoes, allowing your bare feet to connect with the earth. As your toes sink into the cool sand, you feel a surge of energy from the ground. This simple act of removing the barrier between you and the earth helps to neutralize the buildup of positive charge in your body, reducing stress and inflammation.

You practice mindful observation, noticing the gentle lapping of waves, the rustle of leaves, and the gradual shift of colors in the sky. This grounding exercise, both literal and metaphorical, washes away the day's stress, demonstrating how observation and connection to nature can be powerful tools for maintaining calm in chaotic situations.

A hidden treasure ignites your sense of wonder.

N - Nurture: In a hidden cove, you discover a weathered wooden box partially buried in the sand. Curious, you gently open it to find a glass bottle containing a cryptic message and a partial map. As you unfold the fragile paper, you feel a surge of excitement. The message reads: "To unlock the secrets of the lake, follow the path of twilight's wake." This unexpected discovery ignites your sense of adventure and curiosity. You realize how rejuvenating it feels to engage in this spontaneous treasure hunt, feeding your soul's need for exploration and mystery. You contemplate how nurturing your sense of wonder might provide resilience when facing life's challenges.

A moment of self-care nourishes body and mind.

N - Nourish: The map leads you to a small clearing where you find a campfire already set up, with a kettle of water just beginning to boil and an assortment of herbal tea bags waiting. As you select a soothing blend and prepare your tea, you notice another clue etched into a nearby stone: "Nourish body and mind, for the journey ahead is one of a kind." While sipping the warm, flavorful brew, you reflect on how this act of self-care can significantly impact your evening wind-down. How might these nourishing practices, combining adventure with mindful preparation, sustain you during demanding times?

Gentle exercise invigorates the body and sharpens the mind.

E - Exercise: Energized by the tea and the mystery, you follow the next clue on your map, which leads you on a gentle walk along the shore. Physical activity invigorates you, underscoring how light exercise can be a perfect component of an evening routine.

As you walk, you discover markers left by the mysterious message sender, each one encouraging you to perform a simple stretch or yoga pose. This combination of movement and mindfulness not only exercises your body but also sharpens your mind for the puzzle ahead.

Quiet contemplation reveals patterns and insights.

C - Contemplate: The trail leads you to a quiet meditation spot overlooking the lake. Here, you find a journal with a note: "Reflect on your journey, both today and beyond." As you gaze out over the water, you take time to process the day's events, your progress in solving the mystery, and your broader life goals. This moment of contemplation helps you recognize patterns in your behavior and decision-making, providing valuable insights for crafting your 24-Hour Blueprint.

Gratitude ripples outward, creating far-reaching effects.

T - Thank: The final clue brings you to a small altar-like structure near the water's edge. On it, you find smooth stones and an invitation to practice gratitude: "For each thing you're thankful for, place a stone in the water." As you perform this ritual, watching the ripples spread from each stone, you reflect on how gratitude can create far-reaching effects in your life. This practice fills you with positivity, and you wonder how it might serve as a beacon of hope during challenging times.

An unexpected challenge tests your newfound skills.

Just as you're basking in this serene moment, the sky darkens unexpectedly. A gentle rain begins to fall, rippling the once-still lake. This sudden change presents a challenge: how will you maintain your evening routine and positive mindset in the face of this literal and metaphorical storm?

Adapting the CONNECT framework to face life's storms.

Drawing on the lessons you've learned, you see this rain not as a disruption but as an opportunity to apply your CONNECT skills in a new context.

You take shelter under a nearby tree and begin to adapt:

1. **Connect:** You imagine sharing this moment with a loved one, planning to describe this experience to them later.
2. **Observe:** You focus on the unique sensations of the rain - its sound, smell, and feel - practicing mindfulness.
3. **Nurture:** You use this unexpected quiet time to mentally work on a personal project or goal.
4. **Nourish:** The rain becomes a symbol of refreshment, reminding you to hydrate and care for yourself.
5. **Exercise:** You do some gentle stretches under the tree's

canopy.

6. **Contemplate:** The rhythm of the rain provides a backdrop for deeper reflection.

7. **Thank:** You find gratitude in this moment, appreciating nature's unpredictability and your ability to adapt.

The journey itself becomes the treasure.

As you complete this mini adventure, you realize that the journey itself was the treasure, teaching you valuable lessons about curiosity, self-care, physical well-being, reflection, and gratitude. These experiences have brought the CONNECT framework to life in a tangible, memorable way, preparing you for the challenges and opportunities that lie ahead in crafting YOUR 24-HOUR BLUEPRINT.

A sense of completion washes over you.

As you place the final stone of gratitude into the water, a sense of completion washes over you. The message in the bottle, the map, and the clues you've followed throughout the evening have all served their purpose. You take a moment to reflect on the journey, the lessons learned, and the connections made.

The final challenge awaits: Crafting your 24-Hour Blueprint.

You realize that this entire evening adventure has been preparation for the final challenge: crafting YOUR 24-HOUR BLUEPRINT. Each element of the CONNECT framework – from the grounding observation by the lakeshore to the gratitude practice at the water's edge – has provided you with invaluable insights into how to structure your ideal day.

Taking a deep breath of the crisp night air, you feel a profound sense of readiness. You've not only learned about the components of a fulfilling evening routine but experienced them in a deeply personal way. This journey has shown you the power of intentionality, the importance of balance, and the impact of mindful transitions throughout your day.

Transformed, you stand ready to shape your time with purpose.

With newfound clarity and purpose, you're prepared to take on the challenge of designing your own 24-Hour Blueprint. You know that this task will require you to synthesize all you've learned throughout "The Power of 24 Hours" – from the RISE Framework for your mornings to the FOCUS Framework for productive work, from the TIME Mastery techniques to the PEAKS Protocol for sustainable performance, and now the CONNECT Framework for rejuvenating evenings.

As you leave the lakeside, you carry with you not just the memory of this enriching evening, but a toolkit of experiences and insights ready to be applied to your life. The journey through "The Power of 24 Hours" has transformed you from someone who merely experiences time to someone who can shape it with purpose and intention.

The path to true time mastery lies ahead.

With anticipation building, you're ready to begin the final chapter of your journey. It's time to craft a blueprint that will guide you through any type of day with intention and purpose, adapting to your needs while keeping you aligned with your goals. The path to true time mastery lies ahead, and you're prepared to take the first step.

How will you use the insights gained from this evening adventure to shape your ideal day? Turn the page to begin crafting YOUR 24-HOUR BLUEPRINT, the culmination of your journey through "The Power of 24 Hours."

YOUR 24-HOUR BLUEPRINT

The 24-Hour Blueprint is more than just a daily schedule—it's an integrated approach to time mastery that integrates all the frameworks you've learned throughout this book. As you begin this chapter, recall the glowing blueprint you witnessed at the lake.

How can you infuse that same sense of purpose and intentionality into your own 24-Hour Blueprint?

Let's break down how each component contributes to your ideal day:

1. **RISE Framework**: Your blueprint begins the moment you open your eyes. This crucial first phase of your day sets the tone for everything that follows. Here's how to incorporate the RISE Framework into your morning:

- **Revitalize:** Start with activities that energize your body and mind. This could include light exercise, stretching, or deep breathing exercises.
- **Infuse:** Fill your morning with purpose by revisiting your goals and setting intentions for the day.
- **Strategize:** Create efficient morning routines that eliminate decision fatigue and save time for what matters most.
- **Execute:** Incorporate activities that uplift your mood and mindset, such as gratitude practices or motivational reading.

Your blueprint should outline a morning routine that not only prepares you for the day ahead but also aligns with your long-term goals and values.

Remember how you felt when you first stepped into the lake scene, grounded and observant. How can you incorporate that same sense of presence into your morning routine?

1. **FOCUS Framework**: With a strong start from your RISE routine, your blueprint then incorporates periods of deep focus. This section of your day is where you'll make significant progress on your most important tasks. Here's how to maximize your focus:

- Frame: Set up your environment and mindset for deep work. This might involve creating a distraction-free workspace or using specific cues to signal it's time to focus.
- Optimize: Identify your peak productivity hours and allocate your most important tasks to these times.
- Challenge: Push yourself with tasks that are slightly beyond your current abilities to promote growth and engagement.
- Understand: Recognize the signs of flow state and learn how to cultivate it more consistently.
- Sustain: Use techniques like the Pomodoro method or time-blocking to maintain focus over extended periods.

Your blueprint should include strategies for entering deep focus, maintaining concentration, and warding off distractions. Remember, these periods of intense focus are where you'll make the most significant strides towards your goals.

1. **MOTIVATE Framework**: Your blueprint must include strategies to maintain high motivation throughout the day. Here's how to incorporate the MOTIVATE Framework:

- **Map out small steps:** Break down larger goals into manageable tasks.

- **Objective setting:** Establish clear, compelling goals for each day.
- **Time-bound commitments:** Set deadlines to create a sense of urgency.
- **Identify and acknowledge:** Recognize obstacles and challenges.
- **Validate and assess:** Regularly evaluate your progress and methods.
- **Adjust and adapt:** Be flexible in your approach as circumstances change.
- **Take action and evaluate:** Implement your plans and review the results.
- **Energize with inspiration:** Regularly reconnect with your core motivations.

Your blueprint should include regular motivation check-ins and strategies to reignite your drive when it wanes.

1. **TIME Mastery Framework:** To ensure continuous improvement, your blueprint will incorporate the TIME Mastery Framework:

- **Track:** Regularly monitor how you spend your time.
- **Investigate:** Analyze patterns in your productivity and time use.
- **Map out:** Align your actions with your goals and values.
- **Execute:** Implement strategies based on your insights.

Include regular check-ins in your blueprint to refine your approach and ensure your time management evolves with your changing needs and goals.

1. **THRIVE Framework:** Balance is key to sustainability. Your

blueprint will incorporate elements of the THRIVE protocol throughout your day:

- **Transform:** Continuously improve your routines for peak performance.
- **Harmonize:** Align your actions with your goals and values.
- **Revitalize:** Implement strategies to maintain high energy levels.
- **Investigate:** Regularly analyze your productivity patterns.
- **Visualize:** Use mental imagery to enhance performance and motivation.
- **Execute:** Take focused, intentional action towards your goals.

Integrate these elements into your blueprint to ensure high performance without burnout.

1. **CONNECT Framework:** As your day winds down, your blueprint guides you through meaningful evening routines:

- **Connect:** Engage meaningfully with loved ones.
- **Observe:** Practice mindfulness and self-awareness.
- **Nurture:** Engage in activities that feed your soul.
- **Nourish:** Provide proper care for your body and mind.
- **Exercise:** Incorporate light physical activity.
- **Contemplate:** Reflect on your day and set intentions.
- **Thank:** Practice gratitude for the day's experiences.

Your 24-Hour Blueprint isn't rigid—it's a flexible framework that adapts to your needs while keeping you aligned with your goals. Some days may require more focus on work, others on personal development or relationships. The power of your blueprint lies in its ability to guide you through any type of day with intention and purpose.

By integrating all these frameworks, your blueprint becomes a comprehensive system for time mastery. It's not just about managing your schedule, but about optimizing your energy, maintaining focus, aligning with your goals, fostering connections, and adapting to life's inevitable curveballs.

In the following sections, we'll walk through the process of creating your personalized blueprint. You'll assess your current patterns, align your activities with your goals, and learn to implement this blueprint in a way that feels natural and sustainable.

Remember, this isn't about perfection—it's about progress. Your 24-Hour Blueprint is a powerful tool for transformation, but it's also a work in progress. As you grow and evolve, so will your blueprint. The journey to time mastery is ongoing, and with this blueprint in hand, you're well-equipped for the road ahead.

As you begin to envision your ideal 24-Hour Blueprint, you're on the cusp of a transformative experience. The journey you've undertaken through "The Power of 24 Hours" has equipped you with a wealth of knowledge and strategies. Now, it's time to put it all together and create a day that truly aligns with your goals, values, and aspirations.

In the final adventure that awaits you, "The Nexus of Time Mastery," you'll have the opportunity to see how all these pieces fit together in a dynamic, immersive experience. This adventure will challenge you to apply everything you've learned, from the RISE Framework to the CONNECT Framework and everything in between.

As you prepare for this culminating experience, consider:

How have your perceptions of time changed since beginning this journey? What strategies have resonated most strongly with you? Where do you still see room for growth in your time mastery skills?

The Nexus of Time Mastery will be more than just a test of your skills – it will be a celebration of how far you've come and a glimpse into the potential that awaits you. It's an opportunity to see your 24-Hour Blueprint come to life in ways you might never have imagined.

Approach this final adventure with an open mind and a willingness to push your boundaries. The insights you gain here will be the final pieces of the puzzle, helping you to fully realize the power of your 24 hours.

Are you ready to step into the Nexus of Time Mastery? Turn the page when you're prepared to embark on this final, transformative adventure. Your journey to true time mastery awaits!

Beyond the 24th Hour

YOUR JOURNEY CONTINUES

As you turn the final page of "YOUR 24-HOUR BLUEPRINT," a profound sense of accomplishment washes over you. This is more than just finishing a book; you have completed a transformative journey. For a moment, you sit in silence, letting the weight of this realization settle in.

You Enter a Nexus of Time.

You close your eyes, taking a deep breath, and immerse yourself in reflection. The quiet around you seems to deepen, creating a space for introspection - a personal Nexus of Time Mastery.

"I've come so far," you think, a mixture of pride and awe filling your chest. "From feeling like a victim of time to becoming its master."

Memories of growth flood your mind.

Memories flood in, not as distinct adventures, but as pivotal moments of growth:

The crushing weight of procrastination lifting off your shoulders as you implemented the RISE framework. The exhilaration of your first truly productive morning, powered by the FOCUS techniques. The peace that came with learning to say 'no' to the unimportant, guided by your MOTIVATE strategies. The satisfaction of aligning your actions with your deepest values through the TIME Mastery framework.

Epiphanies reshape your view of time.

As you sit in this space of introspection, epiphanies begin to dawn, each one resonating through your being:

"Time isn't just a resource to be managed," you realize. "It's the very fabric of my life, to be shaped and directed with purpose."

You feel newly empowered.

This thought expands, filling you with a sense of empowerment you've never felt before. You see now that every moment is an opportunity, every hour a chance to move closer to your ideal self.

You become the author of your own story.

"I'm not just managing time," you reflect. "I'm curating my life experience, choosing what deserves my attention and energy."

This revelation brings with it a profound sense of freedom. You're no longer a slave to your schedule or others' expectations. You're the author of your story, writing it one intentional moment at a time.

Courage surges as you embrace the power of choice.

"Every 'no' I say to the unimportant is a resounding 'yes' to what truly matters."

With this, you feel a surge of courage. You see how setting boundaries and making tough choices isn't limiting - it's liberating. It's the key to living a life that's true to your values and aspirations.

Midnight strikes, symbolizing a new beginning.

Standing up, you look at the clock on the wall. It's exactly midnight - the start of a new day, symbolizing the fresh start you're about to embark on. You feel a new energy coursing through you, steady and purposeful.

You craft a plan to implement your newfound wisdom.

Picking up a notebook, you begin to write, capturing the pivotal moments of your journey and outlining your plan for the coming weeks:

- **Week 1:** Implement your personalized morning routine, refining it each day.
- **Week 2:** Focus on deep work sessions, pushing your boundaries of concentration.
- **Week 3:** Practice saying 'no' and realigning your commitments with your true priorities.
- **Week 4:** Fine-tune your time tracking, adjusting based on your insights.

You're ready for future challenges.

You know there will be challenges ahead. Old habits may try to reassert themselves. Unexpected obstacles will arise. But now, you're prepared. You have the skills to adapt, to persevere, to thrive.

A sense of limitless possibility fills you.

Looking out the window at the world bathed in moonlight, you feel a sense of limitless possibility. You're not just managing time anymore - you're shaping your destiny, one intentional hour at a time.

Dawn breaks on your new life.

As the first hints of dawn begin to color the sky, you feel ready to step into this new chapter of your life. You've unlocked the power of your 24 hours, but you realize that the true adventure lies in what you do with that power.

Your journey moves from reading to action.

Your journey doesn't end here - it's just the beginning. With each new day, you can refine your skills, push your boundaries, and live more authentically. You're not just a reader anymore; you're a practitioner, a master in the making.

As you prepare for your first RISE routine of this new era, you make a promise to yourself: to approach each day as a new opportunity for growth, to view each challenge as a chance to apply your skills, and to never stop learning and evolving.

You vow to keep growing.

The world is waiting, full of potential. With your newfound mastery, you're prepared to meet it head-on, to shape it according to your vision. This isn't the end of your journey - it's the beginning of a life lived with intention, purpose, and joy.

You step forward into your new life.

You take a deep breath, center yourself, and step forward into the dawn of your new life. Your mastery of the 24 hours has given you the tools. Now, it's time to build the life you've always dreamed of.

Your journey continues. Make every moment count.

www.ingramcontent.com/pod-product-compliance
Lightning Source LLC
Chambersburg PA
CBHW062103080426
42734CB00012B/2730